# "Train Nonprofit Managers in Big Data

Harold B. Thomas

Abstract

This nonexperimental, survey-based online quantitative study on nonprofit managers'
technical training measures the extent of the influence on big data technology use. The
unified theory of acceptance and use of technology is a theoretical framework to
determine whether business managers are trained to have know-how in using big data
technology. This study followed a quantitative methodology to help narrow the gap in
research between what is not known in relation to the nonprofit manager's technical
training on the use of big data technology. Today's data is the most critical asset, but
progress toward big data technology-oriented usage needs to be accessed by the
nonprofit. Nonprofits need to use big data technology to gain insights into identifying the
program activities and monitor them to make better decisions that maximize societal
impact. Big data technology allows nonprofit managers to be effective by getting insights
into the problem-solving of the social programs where they operate to reduce
unemployment, poverty, social exclusion, and low education levels. This study seeks to
answer how nonprofit managers differ in technical training (facilitating conditions) using
big data technology compared to managers who have not used big data technology to
manage business operations. The study may contribute to bridging existing research gaps
in managers' technical training and using big data technology.

## Table of Contents

## List of Tables

# List of Figures

Chapter 1: Introduction to the Study

Research findings from the unified theory of acceptance and use of technology (UTAUT; Venkatesh et al., 2003) concluded that technical training through facilitating conditions could impact intentions to use technology, particularly big data (Mills & Harris, 2019). Nonprofit managers fulfill the critical business operations goals requiring technical training to support the programs within the available time and resources (Santos, 2021). Nonprofits need to use big data technology to gain insights into identifying the program activities and monitor them to make better decisions that maximize societal impact. Using these programs, nonprofit organizations aim to alleviate the problems of the society where they operate to reduce unemployment, poverty, social exclusion, and low education levels. Nonprofit business managers need guidance in getting the technical training that will enable them to meet the goal orientation in competence, confidence, and capability in using technologies (Indrawati & Khalik, 2020). As a result of training interventions, nonprofit managers are incentivized to learn the technology that can be a potential enabler in building knowledgeable business managers who emulate and deliver on the organization's mission (Duan & Deng, 2021). Chapter 1 introduces the section on the background of the study and describes the training and adopting big data technology. Chapter 1 includes the problem statement, purpose, research question and hypothesis, theoretical foundation, study nature, definitions, assumptions, scope and delimitations, limitations, and the study's significance. The end of the chapter has a summary and transition.

## Background of the Study

This quantitative study is to identify how technical training for managers in nonprofit organizations may affect their understanding of big data technology utilization (Peñarroja et al., 2019). As technologies evolve, the manager's ability to learn and acquire new skills and expand their capabilities through training is vital (Persaud, 2021). Hence, there is an urgent need to understand the impact of training in the fast-changing era of big data technology in the labor market (Fritsch et al., 2021). Technological advancements disrupt the managers' knowledge, threatening unemployment and making professionals obsolete in the workforce. In keeping up with the emerging technologies, the nonprofit must assist business managers in learning new skills and knowledge to get insights that measure and quantify the programs (Sudatta et al., 2021). Big data technology can address and evaluate various nonprofit programs related to hunger, disease, poverty, and social inequity (White et al., 2019).

Nonprofits should implement big data technology techniques, providing managers with the conditions to know and use these techniques to obtain information and make decisions that allow monitoring of the program outcomes (Mayer, 2019). In the same way, nonprofits should back the training for managers with technology techniques to avoid the resistance to using big data from the suspicion that managers fear or risk using an unknown technology. To effectively learn adaptable and buildable skills, nonprofit business managers should receive timely and appropriate updated training in big data realized technology (Papa et al., 2021). Using the training, nonprofit organizations may help managers locate valuable information using big data technologies, which minimize potential errors in programs (Cabrera-Sánchez & Villarejo-Ramos, 2020). Big data technologies are adopted more rapidly when training conditions are in place (Queiroz & Pereira, 2019).

The UTAUT suggested that training may accelerate the intention to use technology when implementing a new system by considering the perceived business manager's compatibility skills, and technical training is crucial. Nonprofits without resources, knowledge, and management support on technology training would likely defer the implementation of big data technologies. Perceived support from the organization for sanctioning required training resources gives rise to the possibility of adopting and implementing big data technology (Md et al., 2020).

To fill the research gap is to determine whether a relationship exists between the independent variable technical training and the dependent variable use of big data technology. It requires technical support, education, training resources, and opportunities to support technological advancement (Chin et al., 2019). Nonprofits with training provide awareness of big data technology with a clear purpose and benefits for the managers to experience activities aligned with their enterprise's social mission. Without big data technology, the use of data typically requires more training and education, that is, finding the correct program information efficiently by spending a significant amount of time searching, filtering, and probing; (Chin et al., 2019).

The facilitating condition comprises a user environment with adequate technical training support for big data technology. Several previous studies have also described the same thing regarding the possibility of facilitating conditions on training that may have increased the intention to use technology (Venkatesh et al., 2003) and are based on theoretical explanations and empirical evidence (Respati et al., 2021). The facilitation conditions on training are the support nonprofits provide to managers that can impact the use and adoption of technology. The facilitating conditions include supporting staff skills and implementing training to promote big data technology (Peñarroja et al., 2019).

Facilitating conditions refer to the availability of training resources and education that influences the ability to learn technologies. In contrast, a lack of learning resources is a barrier that can affect the manager's ability to adopt technology (Jarvie-Eggart et al., 2021). Nonprofits providing education to meet the training requirements on big data technology will enhance skills in performing complex tasks and reaching objectives to increase managers' knowledge in doing a job. Practical training is most significant in the workplace to make the managers skilled towards attaining their job and becoming resourceful. Adequate training and equal opportunities must provide personal development in every employee's job. Whenever a need for knowledge requests arises, it is necessary to update the managers' knowledge and skill through practical training (Bammidi & Hyndhavi, 2019).

According to Nelson (2020), the future needs of nonprofit managers would be in business management that requires meeting social missions. Training in information technology is critical to achieving the program goals and the process where managers can learn about the demands of big data technology within a short time. Because nonprofits lack the big data technology capabilities to deliver programs, they even face challenges during COVID-19 and, as a result, rapidly catch up by trying to build technology capabilities to operate (Loomis, 2020). In this decade, nonprofits must proactively improve their training through better learning to achieve program goals (Miković et al., 2020). According to Venkatesh et al. (2008), the organization must provide adequate knowledge no matter how experienced managers use technology.

## Problem Statement

The situation or issue that prompted the search in the literature is whether managers within nonprofit organizations have sufficient technical training supported to adopt big data technologies (Peñarroja et al., 2019). Nonprofit organizations face capacity deficits that impede their ability to manage data, track outcomes, and assess program effectiveness. Studies have shown that many nonprofit organizations evaluate their programs, and even fewer have business managers who may not be trained with evaluation experience (Shapiro & Oystrick, 2018). Managers who cannot create sustainable and measurable solutions using big data technology require help assessing, monitoring, and implementing programs, which may lead to failures (De Rezende et al.,2019). The lack of proper training that supports nonprofit managers leads to the inability to keep their community-oriented programs viable (Gong & Janssen, 2021).

According to Harris et al. (2018), researchers have investigated this topic but have yet to study it in detail. Therefore, a gap exists in the current 3-5 years of peer-reviewed literature on whether nonprofit business managers are trained, leading to an understanding of using big data technology to manage business operations. Adopting big data technology often needs more understanding and acceptance due to its legacy practices (Chauhan & Sood, 2021). To fill the research gap is to determine whether a relationship exists between the independent variable technical training and the dependent

variable use of big data technology. As Yang and Bayapu (2019) described, the fast

evolution of big data technologies left little time for academic investigation. Although

researchers have investigated the topic, it needs to be fully explored; a gap exists in the

current peer-reviewed research literature on empirical findings on business managers'

viewpoints toward big data technology adoption and training (Harris et al., 2018). Since

Venkatesh et al.'s (2003) UTAUT model has been extensively utilized in business (Cao

et al. 2021), this study has used UTAUT's constructs. The specific problem is that

nonprofit business managers have not been trained to use big data technology to manage

business operations (Amina, 2021).

**Purpose of the Study**

This nonexperimental, survey-based online quantitative study on nonprofit

managers' technical training measures the extent of the influence on the use of big data

technology (Persaud, 2021). The independent variable is training, and the dependent

variable is using big data technology. The target population in this study consists of

nonprofit managers who may use big data technology for digital power transformation

throughout the United States. Kevin et al. (2019) described that businesses and

educational institutions must work together to determine how best to prepare business

managers for a data-driven era. It is up to schools and universities to provide education

guidance that influences the adoption of data within organizations, allowing program

insight that will drastically change the course of business and alter the usage of the tools

within the organization that is necessary to survive in this highly competitive environment (Cabrera-Sánchez & Villarejo-Ramos, 2020). Adequately using big data will help nonprofits in their programs to locate valuable information, and nonprofits need to use big data to become data-driven, allowing for being content-centric in the age of digital transformation in the United States (McCosker et al., 2022).

## Research Question and Hypotheses

The study will address the following research questions and hypotheses:

Research question - How do nonprofit managers differ in technical training (facilitating conditions) using big data technology compared to managers who have not used big data technology to manage business operations?

$H_0$: Nonprofit managers differ in technical training (facilitating conditions) do-not-use big data technology to manage business operations.

$H_a$: Nonprofit managers differ in technical training (facilitating conditions) do-use big data technology to manage business operations.

## Theoretical Foundation

The study's theoretical concept includes the framework constructs of the UTAUT (Venkatesh et al., 2003) between the independent variable is technical training (facilitating conditions) to examine the dependent variable is the use of big data technology. This study explains the business manager's perspective on technical training (facilitating conditions) to predict the relationship with big data technology (Chorfi et al., 2022). The UTAUT model (Venkatesh et al., 2003) remains narrowly focused on the evaluation described by Queiroz and Pereira (2019). UTAUT is an authoritative and mature theory to study user acceptance and use of technology within the theoretical framework. In contrast, according to Sharma et al. (2019), the researchers relied on model comparisons to benchmark the UTAUT, and the framework aimed to assess the influences on the use and adoption of technology. Grover et al. (2020) described building a rationale or theoretical logic for anticipated relationships that allows navigating between the specific problem and the research question that helps keep the research grounded. Allowing for the development of knowledge on big data is valuable for academia and nonprofits. The study focuses on the UTAUT framework, which is widely used to predict relationships between the UTAUT variables (Harris et al., 2018). From a theoretical perspective, the UTAUT framework is the groundwork that provides a lens to examine nonprofit business managers who are provided training and may be enabled to accept new technologies and understand the use of big data (Khin & Kee, 2022).

## Nature of the Study

This nonexperimental, survey-based online quantitative study includes technical training (facilitating conditions) as the independent variable and big data technology use as the dependent variable (Venkatesh et al., 2003). The research design involves a plan to respond to the research problem within the UTAUT theoretical framework (Venkatesh et al., 2003). A structured survey instrument based on UTAUT was provided to participants for data collection. I have received written permission to use this published instrument as described in (see Appendices A and B) survey instrument to adapt (Queiroz & Pereira, 2019). The data collection in a survey questionnaire examines whether Venkatesh et al.'s (2003) UTAUT independent variable, technical training, predicts the dependent variable's use of big data technology that was defined by conducting correlation and linear regression. In this nonexperimental design, the independent variable is not manipulated, and the participants are random, allowing me to measure and understand the statistical analysis. This study involves a quantitative correlational research design to investigate relationships between the independent variable technical training and the dependent variable use of big data technology. Addressing the research problem with a gap in the current findings within 3-5 years of peer-reviewed research literature revealed the specific problem that nonprofit business managers are not trained to use big data to manage business operations. A statistical calculation was conducted on the data gathered from the survey participants to test the hypothesis, allowing me to observe whether or not the $p$ value is less than the selected alpha level that indicates the test fails to reject the null hypothesis (Maennig et al.'s 2022). Two researchers on big data, Cabrera-Sánchez and Villarejo-Ramos (2019), indicated that the UTAUT model must continue to evolve to provide better explanations for the acceptance of new technologies. Future research on big data should seek to identify adoption and use. The second research by Queiroz and Pereira (2019) described this exciting finding opens an opportunity to explore the technology use supported by the literature on big data within the UTAUT. These researchers conducted work based on big data technology that is desirable for the business to gain visualization, value in decision making, and efficiency in their programs.

For the planned research design, the survey was collected from nonprofit managers throughout the United States on big data technology to focus on research-based information described in the survey questions. The online survey was performed using the SurveyMonkey platform, a cloud-based tool that helped me to gather the data from the target population (Miftarević & Paliaga, 2021). The survey questions align with the research question that has allowed interpreting based on a 7-point Likert scale rating. This research has adopted the same Likert scale used by Queiroz and Pereira (2019), as well as adapted their research instrument, where the responses were recorded on a 7-point Likert scale (1 = *strongly disagree* to 7 = *strongly agree*). Knabke and Olbrich (2018) described that the responses received from the survey would be arranged in a non-dichotomous rating scale, allowing the responses from the survey participants to average in a standardized manner for quantitative analysis and to validate the results. The research responses were analyzed to determine the extent of measures associated with the technology training and the intent to use and adopt the big data within the UTAUT construct.

## Definitions

The definitions used are the nonprofit manager's intent to use and adopt big data technology within the nonprofit organization.

- *UTAUT*: Unified Theory of Acceptance and Use of Technology (Venkatesh et al., 2003).

- *Facilitating conditions*: Facilitating conditions are defined as the degree to which an individual believes that an organization's training infrastructure exists to support big data technology (Venkatesh et al., 2003).

- *Technical training*: Technical training is described as the construct of the facilitating condition, which is learning to use big data technology in the workplace (Venkatesh et al., 2003).

- *Big Data technology*: This technology can bring benefits, applications, and uses to nonprofits, especially when making data-based decisions to meet the social mission (Villarejo-Ramos et al., 2021).

- *Use and adapt*: In acceptance of technology, the intention to use reflects a user's desire to use big data technology (Venkatesh et al., 2003).

- *Skill:* Skills are capabilities to empower the knowledge of nonprofit managers with big data competency to understand the social mission (Hsia-Ching et al., 2019).

- *Learning:* Big data technology provides nonprofit managers with easy-to-access information that accelerates learning and opportunities to practice what they learn (Park et al., 2021).

**Assumptions**

The examination of the nonprofit manager's intent to use and adopt big data technology in this study is based on assumptions. Nonprofit managers with a software engineering, information technology, and business management background were expected to answer easy-to-follow closed-end survey questionnaires that offered a clear direction where the quality candidate could provide measurable results. The participants needed to have a basic knowledge of big data and technology adoptions (Qin et al., 2020). When the users need more time for training and encounter complex problems concerning big data functioning, they might generate less intention to use the technology (Chorfi et al., 2022). The assumptions will assist in confirming the credibility and dependability of the study.

## Scope and Delimitations

The quantitative study identifies how nonprofit managers' technical training (facilitating conditions) may affect understanding of big data technology use (Peñarroja et al., 2019). The study used the UTAUT, Venkatesh et al.'s (2003) framework, by investigating whether the nonprofit managers provided with technical training through facilitating conditions help to adopt big data technology. The study scope is not designed to be longitudinal research involving a population sample studied at intervals to examine how time has affected the studied variable and repeatedly examined by the same participants to detect any changes. The sample population of nonprofit managers represents the target population focusing on big data technology use that this study intends to examine. The random collection of surveys from the target population ensures that the sample represents a generalization of the target population (Beaumont & Émond, 2022). It is based on random sampling to recruit readily available online survey participants with the expectation that they are senior executives, information technology managers, or business managers throughout the United States in the nonprofit industry. This study analyzes the collected data and concludes with the survey results. In addition, peer-reviewed literature on nonprofit managers on big data has been examined over the past 5 years. Nonprofit managers who receive training may evolve their skill sets alongside learning enabled by facilitating conditions that may help to use big data technology (Khin & Kee, 2022). The boundaries resulting from this study are pivotal in purposively focusing on the research problem. The study reflects the intentions of nonprofit managers since the study took place in nonprofit organizations, so the findings do not represent managers for-profit.

**Limitations**

The limitation of the study includes outdated management practices that need to be aligned with the great potential to use big data technology in improving business capabilities (Delgoshaei et al., 2019). A visible challenge or bias in management today includes issues related to change, as there are differences between new and old ways of thinking, people, and technology capabilities (Shahbaz, 2019). Discussing improvements allows consideration of new technologies and methods that reduce the need for knowledge of old methods (Haamann & Basten, 2019). SurveyMonkey is a highly respected source for gathering research data from survey participants. All participants are assumed to answer inclusion truthfully and are fully qualified to participate in the survey. It may be more appropriate to survey business managers from nonprofit organizations to address this limitation in the future. Demographic data were collected from the survey participants, and the data were not the focus of the study that includes unknown characteristics of some of the demographics collected may have a modifying effect on either the independent or dependent variables. The limitation of this study on nonprofit manager knowledge of big data technology was overcome by targeting nonprofit managers in SurveyMonkey with prior knowledge of big data technology. This non-experimental research focuses on providing descriptive results rather than establishing a cause-effect relationship. Therefore, non-experimental studies are used for observations (Pérez, 2020).

## Significance of the Study

Positive social change depends on a better understanding of society's insights from the perspective of nonprofit managers using advanced technology adoption of big data with the actual strength and direction of technical training (facilitating conditions). In this study, I examined the strength of the UTAUT constructs. The examination was necessary because big data knowledge gained through technical training may help nonprofit managers to integrate technology into their daily activities, which allows for monitoring the programs. The programs lead to adequate transparency and public trust, and complex solving problems generate more significant value for society. The findings of this study may contribute to nonprofit managers with big data usage in monitoring the programs in business operations, including optimizing workflows, reducing processing time, enhancing business with updated information, and computing capabilities to make critical decisions to meet the social mission. Big data theory justifies further research because big data technology is a better-defined research domain, and studies are based on principal contributions to scientific discussion. With the help of big data technology, the researcher will generate valuable insights from the research that may benefit nonprofit organizations and produce evidence that provides positive outcomes. Nonprofits investing in big data technology may find valuable support from the results (Pospiech & Felden, 2016).

### Significance to Theory

Using the UTAUT, whether nonprofit managers accept and use big data technology is still being determined. Therefore, to fill the research gap, I sought to determine whether there were relationships between big data technology facilitating conditions and technical training that may influence the decisions on using and adopting the technology. The well-established framework of the UTAUT served as a baseline for research on key determinants of the intention to use as Cabrera-Sánchez and Villarejo-Ramos (2019) described technology adoption by companies and consumers as critical for success.

Technology adoption theories have been developed and tested, including the theory of planned behavior and the technology adoption model. UTAUT (Venkatesh et al., 2003) is the most thorough and widely used to predict technology adoption that integrates previous models and theories to predict technology adoption and acceptance. The UTAUT theorizes the relationships that apply to contexts and potentially meaningful relationships in constructs of dependent and independent variables. The UTAUT helps to examine managers in nonprofits who use big data differ in technical training (facilitating conditions) compared to managers who have not used big data.

**Significance to Practice**

In this study, UTAUT is utilized to understand the nonprofit manager's intention to utilize and adopt big data. The results are pivotal in helping nonprofit managers accomplish their goals efficiently by improving operations. Thus, the perceived effectiveness of big data technology aims to show better results to nonprofit business management. According to Swain and Cudmore (2018), UTAUT offers a compelling insight into the factors that drive their technology adoption decisions. This study demonstrated its potential to gain new ground in understanding a given technology measure using the data gathered from the survey and then predicted the difficult adoption intentions for technology. In addition, it helps determine to what extent nonprofit managers believe using big data technology in business operations will help achieve the goals. Ultimately, by providing a greater understanding of the facilitating conditions in technical training for adapting to big data technology, the findings of this study may enable the nonprofit to align the mission and vision to achieve its goals.

**Significance to Social Change**

The nonprofit managers' positive social change in adopting big data technology utilizing facilitating conditions on technical training improves data-informed decision-making in the programs that enhance skill, accountability, management knowledge, and job satisfaction. White et al. (2019) describe the effect on people in communities as due to an action, an activity resulting from a nonprofit project, or a program offering a collective decision on society's well-being Shokouhyar et al. (2018) described the social influence involves in social change. The impact of social influence on social networks suggests that social influence can change the perceptions of social networks, users' values, and willingness to participate in the network. Positive social change involving big data adoption leads to data-informed decision-making, collectively forming business stability that impacts employment, economy, and overall societal well-being.

**Summary and Transition**

The research problem addressed through this study is that nonprofit managers are not trained to use big data technology to manage business operations. In the quantitative study, I sought to determine the differences in technical training (facilitating conditions) to examine nonprofit managers' use of big data technology. The theory and concepts that ground this study include the framework constructs of the UTAUT (Venkatesh et al., 2003), which explains the adequate technical training and presents the manager's perspective that examines the relationship in the intent to use and adopt big data technology. The study aims to show that technical training (facilitating conditions) may influence big data technology adoption, where lack of training is a critical barrier to adopting big data technology. In the adoption, management support, technical training, and technology skills are potential vital enablers in nonprofits. In Chapter 2, the literature sources are reviewed to identify the gap that the research addressed by providing a critical assessment of prior research on nonprofit managers using big data with the organizational support of facilitating conditions leading to training (Venkatesh et al., 2003).

Chapter 2: Literature Review

This quantitative study examines the gap in the current 3–5 years of peer-reviewed research literature of empirical findings (Khechine et al., 2020). This chapter begins with critically assessing the literature review relevant to address the research problem that managers in nonprofit organizations are not trained and supported by facilitating conditions that may affect their understanding of big data use. Previous researchers have applied the UTAUT framework (Venkatesh et al., 2003), and many studies have used the technology adoption theory in multiple scenarios proving that it has the ability to provide explanatory conclusions (Du et al. (2020).

The transformation of management professionals requires a need to have technical training that focuses on forming competencies in understanding the knowledge to adopt technologies (Степанов, 2019). Chapter 2 describes the literature search strategy, the theoretical foundation findings, and an exhaustive literature review. The literature review consists of an in-depth overview of the previously published works with a synthesis of the research within the UTAUT framework from the past 5 years.

**Literature Search Strategy**

Articles selected for this literature review were related to the findings of nonprofit managers with technical training (facilitating conditions) and the use of big data. The keywords searched include *big data, technology, implement, adopt, use, nonprofit, managers, training, system, acceptance, learning, facilitating condition,* and *applicable UTAUT model* (Venkatesh et al., 2003). The search took place within the Walden University library databases, including ABI/INFORM Collection, Thoreau Multi-

Database Search, Business Source Complete, ProQuest Ebook Central, ScienceDirect,

Google Scholar, and related journals. The library search includes peer-reviewed journal

articles, conference papers, books, research papers, magazines, and other materials from

2018 to 2022.

I retrieved relevant scholarly articles from the Walden library databases to answer

this research problem, address the gap, and explain concepts based on applying the

UTAUT theory. The literature study involves a critical review of selected studies that

compares the result of the findings on quantitative methodology examining within the

framework of UTAUT theory that influences the use and adoption of technology. The

Literature Review section contains a critical analysis of academic sources and explains,

summarizes, compares, and contrasts ideas on understanding benefits that lead to the

likelihood of using and adopting data technology. The review enumerates, describes, and

outlines the objectives to evaluate with clarity the previous research and to have a

theoretical lens for the study that helps to determine the nature of the study.

## Theoretical Foundation

The theoretical base for this study is the framework constructs of the UTAUT

(Venkatesh et al., 2003). For this literature review, I conducted a comprehensive

overview of current research that provides a solid foundation for additional knowledge

based on the structured approach within the theoretical framework. The UTAUT model is

empirically compared to eight other models to formulate this unified model. The eight

models reviewed are the theory of reasoned action, the technology acceptance model, the

motivational model, the theory of planned behavior, a model combining the technology acceptance model and the theory of planned behavior, the model of PC utilization, the innovation diffusion theory, and the social cognitive theory (Wedlock et al., 2019). UTAUT was tested using the original data and outperformed the eight individual models (Lawson-Body et al., 2021).

Over the years since its creation, UTAUT has been popularly used as a conceptual perspective for technology adoption and integration analysis by authors who have conducted studies of user adoption of technology. At the time of writing, the main study by Venkatesh et al. (2003) was highlighted more than 30,000 times, and UTAUT was used to address technology adoption (Kumbhar et al., 2021). UTAUT is valuable for researchers to assess the likelihood of success for new technology and helps managers proactively understand interventions that include training targeted populations who may be less inclined to use new technology (Venkatesh et al., 2003). From the research perspective, I need to verify whether the training provided by facilitating conditions influences big data adoption (Queiroz & Pereira, 2019).

Before the UTAUT, the technology acceptance model was used to explain users' acceptance of various types of information and technology, and now with UTAUT is known to be more explainable concerning usage as it overcomes the technology acceptance model's limitations in adoption in an organization setting (Venkatesh et al., 2012). The basic concept underlying UTAUT is that information technology directly predicts actual technology use (Venkatesh et al., 2003). The UTAUT model was developed and formulated in a workplace context (Venkatesh et al., 2003).

The UTAUT model has constructs that can be adjusted to suit scientific study (Sethibe & Naidoo, 2022). The UTAUT (Venkatesh et al., 2003) is adopted as the underlying theoretical lens due to its high explanatory power and robustness in predicting a manager's willingness to use big data technology in a nonprofit organizational setting. It has been shown that UTAUT can help understand the new technology used within a nonprofit organization to design effective interventions (Venkatesh et al., 2003). In this research, the independent variable of technical training (facilitating conditions) and the dependent variable use big data (Chin et al., 2020).

The UTAUT is widely tested and validated across many disciplines and is not just meant for studying information technology adoption. Contrary to the common perception and belief, this theory was also tested in marketing, social psychology, and management. UTAUT can be related to many other theories and frameworks since the theory's nature is quite similar to the others. A vast number of studies across different contexts, integration, and multiple disciplines followed the advancement of UTAUT should serve as the baseline model of future research. Its similarities with other theories and models have positioned it to be a strong core theory and a basis for integration that could be applied to nonprofit organizations (Fadzil et al., 2019).

The UTAUT model provides empirical insight into technology acceptance by comparing prominent technology acceptance theories, which often offer competing or partial perspectives. Domestic and foreign scholars have empirically demonstrated that the UTAUT model is more effective than any previous model, with an explanatory power of up to 70% predictive power (Venkatesh et al., 2003) compared to the rest of the models that examine technology acceptance (Yu et al., 2021). The UTAUT is oriented toward studying information systems designed for organizational use settings and is an appropriate theoretical approach to studying technology adoption (Naranjo-Zolotov, Oliveira, et al., 2019).

UTAUT is suitable for studying complex technology adoption scenarios due to the multiple-way interactions. Moreover, UTAUT considers that information technology may yield valuable insights for theory and practice (Naranjo-Zolotov et al., 2019). Venkatesh et al. (2003) have demonstrated the training (facilitating conditions) as the accessibility of well-functioning technical inevitabilities to permit the user's system handling. From procedural to human support and technical support to organizational support from the perspective of the training atmosphere. Venkatesh et al. (2003) emphasizes technical training availability accept and use systems (Ahmed et al., 2022).

**Literature Review**

The UTAUT (Venkatesh et al., 2003) is one of the extensively utilized technology adoption theories to explain individuals' technology adoption and use by recognizing the opportunities that big data may offer by an increased adoption as a result of facilitating conditions resources on technical training that requires big data-related technology know-how (Sun et al., 2020). Technical training (facilitating conditions) is the degree to which the managers perceive the existence of training resources and support using big data technology whenever necessary. In this context, the facilitation environment with big data technology is available according to the goal and level of participation, for instance, the training resources needed to carry out this task (Naranjo-Zolotov et al., 2019).

The UTAUT technical training (facilitating conditions) links to all the needs that can enable or simplify the practical implementation and a long-term approach, transparency, and total commitment (Castanheira et al., 2019). It has been shown that UTAUT can be a useful managerial tool in understanding the new technology used within an organization to design effective interventions (Venkatesh et al., 2003). The training constructs and efficient infrastructure supports the user's technology (Venkatesh et al., 2003). The facilitating conditions provide technical support for using the learning system in the nonprofit context (Khechine et al., 2020). Researchers have noted the instructional strategies to facilitate effective learning and the adoption extension of the UTAUT model with social impact as a construct implemented to understand the use of technology (Mahara et al., 2021). UTAUT facilitating conditions as a factor can indicate the development of support and training initiatives specifically to promote the uptake of the new technology (Cao et al., 2021). The central aspect relates to developing skills in intelligence and data technology through the technical training of nonprofit managers. Nonprofits should dedicate more to training to enable their professionals, making them qualified to perform more efficiently and effectively, generating insights that add value. Such skills and complementarities are necessary for teams to extract value from the data (Mauricius et al., 2020). The nonprofit connected with information technologies is the staff training corresponding to the current trends in technology, and technological development directly defines the important and significant within society. The technologies in the modern economy significantly result in the change of the nonprofits' requirements and the change of managers' needs for professional competencies of staff.

In the long term, the workforce will impose increased requirements on staff on the possession of professional competencies and interaction with technology in a workplace, including the ability to control and carry out operations and adapt to changes in the competencies (Stepanov, 2019).

Developers of the current modern staff technical training system need to study such professional competencies. In the long term, the result can be a discrepancy in the professional's competence that completed training in the programs of secondary professional education and formed the offer in the labor market to those requirements imposed by employers. In these conditions, the transformation of the staff training system was focused, first of all, on forming those competencies, allowing professionals to use the available equipment and have an opportunity to master new technologies (Stepanov, 2019).

Nonprofits increasingly demand professionals with the skills to analyze program outcomes and derive intelligence from big data. Existing studies have identified a shortage of big data skills as one of the critical problems faced in the 21st century. Big data technology skills are required to describe, predict, diagnose, prescribe, and visualize the complex data generated from various heterogeneous sources. Data that is too complex to be processed by conventional computational systems is called big data. Such data are generated at an excessive amount that tends towards exabytes (volume), exorbitant production rates (velocity), heterogeneity of sources (variety), ability to yield actionable intelligence (value), and the quality of being accurate (veracity) (Nwokeji et al., 2019). These 5Vs define big data. At one end of this spectrum are managers, who are professionals with basic data skills such as creating, interpreting, and using the results of big data to make operational business decisions and perform transactional functions. To gain insight and derive meaningful intelligence from big data, enterprises rapidly demand a broad spectrum of nonprofit managers with big data skill sets. On the other end of the spectrum are experts with an advanced big data skill set and trained in developing program solutions. The demand for big data and skills still excessively exceeds the growing supply (Nwokeji et al., 2019).

The literature indicates that training can be objective, preparing the workers to perform new functions and adapt to new technologies. Therefore, the training is understood to impact the acceptance of new technologies and digital systems. The research on the UTAUT model proposed by Venkatesh et al. (2003) indicates that training is crucial in predicting the acceptance and intention to use new technologies. However, a gap exists in the studies that require investigation between the relationship impact of training and the acceptance of new technologies. Previous research that evaluates the relationship has only used reactions to technical training as a measure and disregarded the assessment of transferring the skills acquired in training to the work context (Farias & Resende, 2020). Then, conducting complete training for the company's employees so that the employees' level of understanding is achieved and met, and a strong commitment from the management regarding the implementation of the system is carried out (Indrawati & Khalik, 2020).

Technological advancements and the industrial revolution have altered the profile of professionals and the relationship between employees and businesses. The fact demonstrated in the field research makes it possible to highlight the knowledge degree of managers about the theme. In Industry 4.0, organizations have already adjusted to the new industrial revolution. Therefore, nonprofits must adapt to the latest market demands by improving, investing in new technologies, and training their employees (Cunha et al., 2020).

The professions are transforming to take advantage of these advanced technologies. Professional training programs must react quickly and appropriately to respond to the shift in knowledge and skills required for the job market and the study enablement professionals to redesign the training curriculum (Chiang et al., 2021). Late adoption of these technologies will affect competitiveness, which will be hard to recover (Bildosola et al., 2020). The importance is to address the training to learn new technologies, and only some studies connect potential training design opportunities. Prior research on UTAUT training possibly impacts reactions and intentions to use technology—mediated by facilitating conditions (Mills & Harris, 2019). Training (facilitating conditions) refers to the degree to which an organizational and technical structure's perceived existence supports the use of technology.

Venkatesh et al. (2003) indicated that training (facilitating conditions) affects technologies positively within the workplace based on the UTAUT model studies. Training positively affects solving technical problems, leading to continuous learning, and the study's findings support improved learning experiences (Lakhal et al., 2020). UTAUT was chosen in the study due to the main added feature, training (facilitating conditions), which is particularly useful in researching educational technology acceptance. Training can indicate the development of support and initiatives to maximize the new learning uptake (Garone et al., 2019).

**Training and Skills**

Nonprofits face digital challenges, and the results highlight that digital transformation, including big data technology, falls into three main pillars. The first pillar is a skill that contains digital education, talents, and culture. The second pillar, training infrastructures and technologies, points out the need for information, interaction, and technology as critical action. The third pillar, ecosystems, highlights the importance of investing in medium- to long-term visions, partnerships, and quality of life (Brunetti et al., 2021). In brief, the study shows that standalone interventions are insufficient to tackle technology from a systemic perspective. This study highlights the importance of developing skills like big data before investing in technical infrastructure and technology. Nonprofits should alter their vision before reconfiguring their business models and invest in smart working, and the study recommends that public administration mainly invests in technology education and partnerships. In contrast, regarding education and training, it suggests providing digital skills to workers (Brunetti et al., 2021). The following are the required skills and knowledge needed to operate in the big data technology environment and the tools provided:

- *Data tools.* The frequency of use reported for these data tools in the workplace is Apache Hadoop HDFS, Apache Hive, Apache HBase, JAQL, Jaspersoft BI Suite, IBM Infosphere, Apache Mahout Machine Learning, and the most frequently used *Tableau Desktop and Server*. Workplace use is lower, except for Tableau software.

- *Statistical tools.* Statistical tools provide needed data transformation analysis. Expertise in statistical analysis is required in dealing with big data. JMP, Minitab, MatLab, SAS, SPSS, Stata, and Statssoft Statistica.

- *Data mining.* Big data allows digging into data using SAS Enterprise Miner, IBM SPSS Modeler, Dryad ParaLLeL Processing, IBM Watson Analytics, R Software, Rapid Miner, and Weka/Pentaho.

- *Data visualization.* Big data visualization tools include Fusion Charts, Google Analytics, IBM Watson Analytics, Microsoft Power BI, Oracle VisuaL AnaLyzer, QlikView, SAP AnaLytics CLoud, and Tableau.

Demand for big data technology continues to escalate, driving a pressing need for managers' skills needed by nonprofits to address the big data needs to be fulfilled by employers (Dolezel et al., 2021). Top big data technologies include Apache Hadoop, MongoDB, RainStor, Cassandra, Presto, RapidMiner, ElasticSearch, Kafka, Splunk, KNIME, Apache Spark, Tableau, and Plotly (Top big data technologies you must know, 2022). Identifying appropriate information from a wide range of data allows nonprofits to make quicker and more rational decisions with the rapid expansion of a large number of available data challenging the current computing infrastructure. The role and effect of big data technology on business decision-making processes and data processing have become a challenge for managers with data sources growth managers face obstacles and opportunities. Nonprofit businesses must be equipped with appropriate skills and aligned with the business strategy to overcome the complexities associated with the business process. The right skills influence nonprofits to use data to transform their operations due to the challenge faced by current managers in identifying and integrating relevant skills that help in effective data-based decision-making in program outcomes. In addition to decision-making skills, an expert skillset is required to support data-based decision-making (Mamabolo et al., 2021).

Nonprofits must adapt to society while slowly developing soft skills that provide collective intelligence while changing their facilitating conditions and employee training. Of course, the digital age has changed the learning process through various stages as big data intervenes to promote better knowledge by focusing on guiding big data and its technology, methods, and tools for learning. It is one of the key factors to increase learning effectiveness that it is evident that each user in a learning platform will follow the process similarly. However, we can choose those that suit them better by diversifying the content broadcast formats, including interactive modules, videos, short, pdf files, quizzes, mini-games, and so forth.

The platforms can also be available on different channels, including web interfaces, mobile applications, and others, to allow access as efficiently as possible and in all circumstances. Also, these platforms can inform learners about their deadlines and the most popular content. Personalizing the learning devices does not seek to define rules that could apply to a category of users and specify how to adapt the learning process. It aims to evaluate the influence of the various parameters (teaching format, time and place of use, rhythm, history, and pedagogical sequences) and implement an evaluation of the quizzes on the choices to predict future decisions (Sedkaoui & Khelfaoui, 2019).

The digital transformation of big data technology requires skills that help business managers thrive to ensure the success of the initiatives. The effort requires that the most significant pillar of digital transformation is that the managers have the right technical and soft skills, are engaged with excellent work, and are empowered to create the digital culture of big data technology. Digital cultures are about ideas, actions, collaboration, flexibility, developing the right skills, and fostering a nonprofit culture ensures digital initiatives' success (Kavanaugh, 2020). Digital initiatives on big data require people with sophisticated technical skills to focus more on creating a superior service experience for the community, where soft skills have become just as important as technical ones. Contrary to technical skills, which have a shelf life, soft skills can improve once developed and practiced where these are inherent foundational skills, as many leaders believe they can be developed with proper training and mentoring. Teamwork has become a particularly high-value skill in the current fast environment where nonprofits must pivot quickly with employees must embrace agile ways of working and collaborating with others across cultures, customs, and time zones. Digital transformation projects are complex, and the success of these projects is hugely dependent on team members exhibiting these qualities (Kavanaugh, 2020).

Leaders build a lifelong learning culture and use it to retain top talent by doing the following:

- pursuing multiple talent approaches and initiatives to meet current needs and prepare for future talent demands,

- providing training programs and teach a lifelong learning tradition,

- having rigorous hiring methods and do not compromise on the quality of hires, but they are open to nontraditional sources, and

- aggressively working toward sustainably more intelligent infrastructures.

Leaders recognize that big data technology is changing how we work and the roles to anticipate these changes and forecast the skills they will need for the next year and beyond. Nonprofits that score high on our readiness index have established forward-thinking processes to hire and develop talents, such as purpose or learning maps that show workers how to get from one skill level to another. Assess workers based on their profiles and work experience and identify and suggest how to rectify skills gaps. Nonprofits should partner with academia strategically and innovatively to jointly develop new talent so education systems and businesses worldwide can keep up with the needs of students or the nonprofits that want to hire them (Kavanaugh, 2020).

Nearly every nonprofit tries to develop the talent it already has, where long-proven approaches such as instructor-led classroom training, onboarding programs, and coaching are widely used. However, while traditional methods of developing talent have only partially fallen by the wayside, learning is becoming more experiential. For example, self-guided online education is just as standard as in-class courses, where nonprofits add digital campuses, boot camps, and hackathons to their skills development offerings and change the speed at which they deliver learning initiatives. The best at developing their managers provide knowledge-sharing platforms, just-in-time online training, and self-guided online learning modules to learn anytime, anywhere, and from any device (Kavanaugh, 2020).

Leaders are more than twice as likely to measure and track their manager's hard and soft skills as a result of their talent development initiatives that allow the implementation of intelligent workplaces also play a role in talent development and retention. The leaders are more likely to create collaborative, sustainable work environments with the latest technology. Nonprofits must move from hierarchical and matrixed structures to team-based, self-managing ones for agile project needs. Digital initiatives require organizational structures that support collaboration and enable managers at all levels to make decisions. Digital initiatives on big data require cooperation, and to allow this, the need to shift from hierarchies to flatter leadership models comprising specialized networks for agility. There is progress in the evolution of team-based structures, and nonprofits are experimenting, yet only some have mastered it at scale. This process requires a culture change that requires leadership guidance, a manager's mindset, human resource transformation, work organization, and management. Every nonprofit culture needs to pilot in small teams and implement the learnings as they look to do it at scale (Kavanaugh, 2020).

There is a need for more challenges when reskilling managers, including a lack of management awareness, support, inadequate talent, and training plans. These barriers are related, as nonprofits consistently undervalue and underfund talent and employee initiatives, ultimately undermining their prospects. Another hurdle for digital big data technology staffing initiatives is an apparent disconnect between senior executives and lower levels of management. Senior leaders believe their nonprofits are better at creating collaborative workspaces and employee experiences than middle management (Kavanaugh, 2020).

Learnability receives short shrift in the survey, which is surprising given the continuous personal and technical development. The market now demands digital talent, which limits the tremendous potential of reskilling, and it can be a competitive advantage for companies that embrace learnability. Undervaluing learnability limits the possibility of other talent initiatives. This narrow mindset of undervaluing learnability is a barrier. It defines the tremendous potential of reskilling, yet it can benefit nonprofits that embrace learnability and lifelong learning. Leaders understand that just teaching skills are not a silver bullet but must also develop the ability to rapidly update their employees' talents in an era of shortening technology cycles. The more managers embrace this understanding, the more likely they will commit to developing the talent they need to compete in the digital era. An essential characteristic of the most successful nonprofit in getting the skills they need is embracing multiple approaches for developing and managing talent and creating the culture to foster digital initiatives (Kavanaugh, 2020).

A good understanding of the social network's activity and dynamics allows for better driving of the learning process. Social learning relies on analyzing social networks to detect communities, identify cohesive subsets, investigate the density, and remember those who help or come up with conflicts related to mutual incomprehension. The precise nature of the data managed by the network and organized around the graph implies defining new adapted measures as the appearance of social networks like Facebook, Twitter, WhatsApp, and other tools. These notions characterize social networks locally and determine their essential elements, such as influencers and intermediaries. The main techniques for detecting communities, or groups on the social network, are based on calculating the connection betweenness. An essential value of this measure suggests that the connection links two different communities (Sedkaoui & Khelfaoui, 2019).

**Knowledge Evidence**

The results highlight the crucial role of independent variable training (facilitating conditions) of UTAUT as influencing factors to show evidence that technology is used at all levels to manage. When the training (facilitating conditions) is benchmarked low, the measures are foreseeable to be challenging to adopt or use new technology because managers form the assessment that tends to rely on the preconceived desire for the targeted system with their developed estimates. It will be less likely to activate a careful prediction of whether to improve training (facilitating conditions) (Mahardika et al., 2019).

Training can allow trainees to improve their knowledge, skills, and abilities, where some researchers use knowledge sharing, knowledge exchange, and knowledge transfer. However, knowledge transfer is any action an individual intends to share or disclose their knowledge. Training is defined as increasing an individual's knowledge to develop the skills and expertise in a particular discipline, such as big data technology, which leads to a change of participants to a specific direction. Poorly trained managers can lead to mistakes, injuries, or even legal involvement problems, which would be more costly than training. Training is a learning experience to permanently change an individual manager's ability to perform an action or job. It involves changing their knowledge, skills, and attitude; generally speaking, it seeks to transfer knowledge and skills to a trainee. In short, training can be seen as a tool for knowledge transfer (Perez-Soltero et al., 2019). Prior research on UTAUT training may impact training reactions and intentions to use technology (Mills & Harris, 2019). Therefore, the companies provide training to supervisors that help to elevate managers' creative self-efficacy, which, in turn, would be expected to result in higher levels of creativity. Like other cognitive processes, dialectical thinking needs to be trained in leaders and followers. Doing so may make them more receptive to creative ideas and more likely to facilitate creative action in others. Nonprofits with creative activities could also consider integrating dialectical thinking into the corporate culture. At the very least, a dialectical mindset as a selection criterion may be appropriate when choosing managers or leaders responsible for teams tasked with creating goals (Han & Bai, 2020).

The nonprofit must educate managers about the usefulness of a technology system and sell the benefits that help understand the importance of technology use and provide thorough training. However, managers may consider it easy to use if they are taught about the navigation and menu before training exercises. In addition, this study also showed that managers' attitudes towards usage could influence their perceptions of knowledge gained and task completion satisfaction, which should help increase the effectiveness and efficiency of the training (Klaus & Changchit, 2020).

Technical training (facilitating conditions) includes supporting staff, promotion, management support, or training implemented to facilitate the use of technology. Managers are more likely to participate in the activities set up to promote the use of the technology, provide specialized instruction to their employees, and ensure that consulting staff are available for assistance (Peñarroja et al., 2019). Additional considerations are addressed to improve the learning, including activation of prior knowledge, demonstration, and application, in other words, letting the user practice problems with increasing difficulty and integrating the learning back into the workplace. Prerequisite knowledge gained and activation support research linking new information to prior knowledge, improving learning, and facilitating transfer (Mills & Harris, 2019).

Technical training involves acquiring information to make knowledge that forms intelligence that allows changing behavior by humans and, increasingly, non-humans. For humans, this can include reflection to reveal values and assumptions, insights into practice, allowing a revision of attitudes, and deciding responsibly and wisely. Nonprofit managers could create, acquire, and transfer knowledge that adapts to unpredictable conditions more quickly than competitors. By accepting and disseminating knowledge, nonprofits can shape their future. Frequently considering tacit knowledge, it is possible that learning can remain hidden or unrecognized. Deliberately or otherwise, by seeing patterns that become possible ideas for application through explanation and sharing through interpreting and emphasizing the need to consider contextual features to enable knowledge sharing and conversion. Leaders and managers can become learning-driven, but learning needs to be critical of assumptions, the values that inform those assumptions, and the consequences of what is done in practice. Because of this, it is essential to investigate learning processes within and beyond traditional boundaries and how such techniques can contribute to nonprofit learning (Garad & Gold, 2019).

Leaders and managers should know their learning approaches, instrumental learning, and communicative learning. Instrumental learning is about controlling and manipulating the environment, improving, and predicting performance, and assessing the truth claims. Communicative learning is about understanding what someone means when communicating, applying awareness, and critiquing assumptions and intentions (Garad & Gold, 2019).

**Resources**

UTAUT theory emerged via reviewing and consolidating eight competing and conceptually similar models (Venkatesh et al., 2003). Findings revealed that facilitating conditions' UTAUT variable is the most influencing variable (Misra et al., 2020). UTAUT holds the construct of technical training (facilitating Conditions), which describes the degree to which participants believe training, support, and background knowledge are available to use the technology. It needs to be initially defined as the belief that nonprofits and technical training infrastructure exist to support the use of the new technology (Garone et al., 2019).

Technical training is a manager's perceived availability of support in the environment, such as access to skills and administrative support, that encourages and facilitates technology acceptance. Training and adequate technical support are barriers to technology integration (Eksail Fuad & Ernest, 2020). Training construct indicates that users require system availability at the workplace and argues that the absence of technological infrastructure for training could demotivate users from adopting the technology. Users must gain the necessary operational skills to reduce the intention to adopt information technology (Rahi et al., 2019).

The relationship in training is mediated by facilitating conditions within the context of technology acceptance. Technical training includes resources or supports that remove burdens that may hinder the acceptance and use of technology in providing technical support to staff, access to system experts, peer mentors, top management support, reference tutorials, and documentation manuals on how to use the system. Technical training is used to capture this information holistically. There appears to be a clear gap in the existing literature that needs to address a growing interest in identifying the impact of training on intentions to use technology in both pre-and post-training settings (Harris et al., 2018).

Defining Industry 4.0 by combining all these systems into a typical architecture involves using a large amount of unstructured, diverse data processed with much greater speed and variety than ever before to evaluate existing technologies and transition to new ones. Processing such data arrays is becoming a problematic separate task for the functioning of a nonprofit in the context of global digitalization, for the solution of which it is logical to use technologies and tools of big data technology. The capabilities of analysis, visualization, and distributed processing software are growing to extract useful information from such data. It also assumes big data technology, which allows for organizing management data correctly and promisingly using an open architecture to integrate internal and external services into the overall management system. An open

system is one whose elements can interact with the external environment (interagency

interaction). Such a system will ensure the formation of architectural aspects of a

nonprofit, considering its learning, mission, and strategy (Martynov et al., 2020). A social

well-being approach is to work more closely with communities, listen to their lived

experiences, and respect better social sector practice. However, advances in big data and

what we can do with technology give new tools and ways of doing things in programs. It

is leading the use of data, and it has the potential to bring about tangible social change.

Now it is up to others to check it out and use it too (Gibson, 2021). Discover the

tendencies and developments that will influence the nonprofit when applying the

concepts of Industry 4.0. It is necessary to recognize the opportunities or changes in the

market to create correct pilot projects that require implementing the vertical integration

that involves mapping resources the nonprofit needs with details. Seek information in a

collaborative environment, risk analysis, and identify and collect data properly by

planning an exosystemic approach. Invest in up-to-date technology, learn to handle

managers' training demands, research, and apply better market standard practices. The

nonprofit must continue competitively in the market by focusing on digital technologies

and training its employees. Digital transformation is intimately connected to the

availability of resources to evaluate data (Cunha et al., 2020).

Nonprofits need to develop vital skills for data, and varied qualifications,

experience in complex algorithm processes, and workflow integration must be available.

Today, big data technology is the leading technology used, and it is necessary to understand its demands and apply the technologies that will offer more benefits (Cunha et al., 2020). Nonprofits often need more clarification about big data adoption and implementation requirements before starting their big data technology initiatives. Developing new big data applications requires that staff program and analyze the data and knowledge. These capabilities can either be developed in-house through training and experimentation or bought on the market and internalized. Knowledge transfer and information flow from internal and external sources are essential in creating dynamic capabilities (Gong & Janssen, 2021).

Technical training courses focus on generic coaching skills rather than those specific to managerial coaching. In addition to covering basic coaching skills, training must include topics such as aligning goals and establishing trust and specific competencies for the team in the coaching context. Despite this demand for tailoring the content of a coaching training program to the nonprofit coaching context where the best practices include pre-training a need analysis from various perspectives such as job and the individual. During the training, finding ways to assist participants in getting into the right mindset and allowing practice opportunities is essential. Post-training, the learning transfer is also necessary, including recommendations for the participant's manager and allowing the new skills to be implemented (Milner et al., 2018).

Nonprofits can start technical or quality training for existing employees to enhance their skills (Baig et al., 2019). Prospective adopters often want to try the technology platform to become familiar with its functionality and observe how it fits into their tasks before adopting it. In this regard, user training programs can give prospective adopters a chance to try and evaluate the technology before deciding to adopt or reject it. The ability to try and observe tools in action provides an excellent way for prospective adopters to reduce uncertainty regarding their perceived benefits and limitations before deciding to adopt them. Identifying and disseminating best practices for inserting technologies into operational environments can also help share and observe the value any specific technique may provide (Mohammad, 2019).

**Managers Perspective**

UTAUT is a theory for investigating the influence of managers in adopting technology. The knowledge and professionalism that includes prior knowledge, training, and expertise influence the adoption. Hence, understanding the impacts enhances the perspective of use. Thus, rather than evaluating users' reactions to IT-enabled technology by testing the significant influence of inputs that includes UTAUT's training (facilitating conditions), it allows an understanding of the impacts of professionals responsible for the effectiveness of adoption (Alamin et al., 2020). Technology is dramatically changing, so managers must recognize that diverse knowledge and skills are needed. Besides, new digital technologies require different skills than prior waves of transformative technologies (Manfreda & Štemberger, 2019).

Consequently, the technical training of creative managers should be based on new educational standards, which provide for a completely new approach involving the development of a society where management education should be based on new modern learning technologies. The manager's learning needs to be synthesized with practice in the economy to benefit from achievements that advance technical standards. UTAUT training (facilitating conditions) can indicate the development of support and training initiatives specifically to promote the uptake of the new technology. Modern information technologies allow solving and, simultaneously, changes that occur in the training of managers with the dramatic change, so managers must recognize that diverse knowledge and skills are needed. Besides, new digital technologies require different skills than prior waves of transformative technologies (Shahbazov, 2019).

Skills and technology knowledge are necessary for success in the workplace. Technical skills are the core for managers and contain the individual's affinity or ability to complete tasks related to widespread knowledge. Their concrete forms are the leading indicators of their expertise. Technology skills are usually very concrete and tangible, and teaching, learning, and even testing them is easy. Other skills include managing and planning projects focused on problem-solving, which means making the right decision under pressure, being a leader and delegating tasks and responsibilities, and having good time management. Hybrid skills include technical and non-technical managers as people with strong technical and adequate business knowledge or vice versa (Tokarčíková et al., 2019).

**Competency**

Today's business environment is changing rapidly, and the pace of change in yesterday's business environment, today's business environment, and tomorrow's business environment reminds us of the speed war. Level measurements of individual skills are also called a measure of effect and measure the ability of the technology to perform its intended function and its ability to solve problems (Lee & Kim, 2020). Much closer collaboration among public institutions, educational institutions, industry, and community organizations is needed to ensure that training programs evolve with the evolving need for skills driven by dynamic technological changes (Persaud, 2021).

Since the advent of big data technology, nonprofits need to adopt and implement and have the availability of data-savvy managers successfully. These are not data analysts but managers that can ask valuable questions, understand the implications of the analysis, and implement program decisions that employ the results of data analysis. Big data technology is the next frontier, and one of the issues for nonprofits is that the demand for big data technology knowledge is greater than the supply (Anderson & Williams, 2019).

The education, training, and development needs are apparent when a manager's nonprofit indicates that a new or improved competency is required. On the other hand, many nonprofits do not provide competency assessments to help people understand how their current performance aligns with future expectations. In those cases, the person must find a way to determine what improvements are needed to ensure future success. For many managers, choosing those opportunities is a challenging assignment. Many issues can undermine the results, such as positive and negative past experiences, personal biases, limited perspectives of workforce trends, and lack of familiarity with technology trends. For instance, Microsoft® designed a comprehensive competency for educators that can be used to guide competency development and improvement. Its website states, "These education competencies represent many of the attributes, behaviors, areas of knowledge, skills, and abilities required for a successful job" (Hopen, 2019). Technology skills consist of a combination of hard and soft big data skills. Hard-big data skills include analytics, programming, artificial intelligence, and machine learning capabilities, whereas soft-big data skills include troubleshooting, learning, customer centricity, collaboration, and goal-centric thinking. Talents that promote a digital-first mindset are critical for any nonprofit to implement technology transformation successfully (Nair et al., 2019).

It consists of training and experience that require the staff to work in complex socio-technical environments. The nonprofit can benefit by using social media to disseminate experiences and lessons learned to provide virtual and augmented learning environments. Allows sharing the expertise that can assist the management system appraisals, implement safety arrangements, connect the worker using the virtual learning experiences, and develop learning management systems. There is a need for a highly skilled workforce to deal with data to make better decisions. Decision-makers can address this issue by training current employees (James, 2021).

Another more significant risk is the wrong team responsible for developing the project. The team plays a vital role in the success of any information technology project. The team is not just the sum of all the professional skills of its managers but, more importantly, the ability to interact with each other. It is essential that each team member clearly understands their role and area of responsibility (Mitrofanova et al., 2019).

Gen X was born between 1965 and 1980 and is the child of Baby Boomers. Online learning, which started in the mid-1990s, offered Gen X learners enhanced learning flexibility and more opportunities than previously available. Growing up with technologies in their classrooms and experiencing opportunities to learn autonomously may explain Gen Xers' preference for flexibility and self-direction in pursuing learning (Lowell & Morris, 2019).

Gen Y is the youngest generation in the workforce, born between 1980 and 1999. The youngest generation is often referred to as Millennials. The oldest Yers were born around the same time as the launch of the personal computer, and these learners are more likely to be comfortable with technology. Gen Yers can be highly motivated to learn if the instruction is engaging and has a specific purpose. These learner characteristics of Gen Yers result in a group of learners who may need to be appealed to differently than training leaders will appeal to other generations (Lowell & Morris, 2019).

Learning preferences and the impact of these learning preferences on technology training are essential factors for training leaders to consider. In addition to generational attitudes and work habits, the teaching techniques, learning experiences, and technologies available during each generational cohort's formative years can be related to cohort members' learning preferences. Generational characteristics move beyond an age distinction of younger vs. older, focusing instead on the aspects of each group as they relate to learning and technology adoption. As our generational identity can impact many things, generational identity should be considered when attempting to address differences in learning and technology preferences between generations (Lowell & Morris, 2019).

**Peer Support**

Peer support is defined as encouragement, giving feedback, or even endorsing the use of new knowledge. Peers with the same knowledge can be used as sparring managers when obstacles in technical usage occur. Awareness of support can be promoted by mediating the role of motivation for peer support in training transfer has been shown as positive for technology training (Richter & Kauffeld, 2020). One concept of dealing with today's uncertain and unpredictable environments is agility. Agility puts people in the center and depends on managers' ability to adapt to change and thrive on it across all hierarchical levels. Recent literature suggests that managers design and effectively implement practices concerning learning and training. Training efforts to enhance agility capabilities need to be dynamic and experienced based. Training participants should have the experience to apply lessons learned, receive feedback, and use them again. Experiential learning and its application within a learning setting enhance agility training (Karre et al., 2020).

**Knowledge Creation**

Evidence from a prior study corroborated that technical training (facilitating conditions) includes community engagement, that is, the nonprofit has a transparent enterprise social network. The use is to provide facilitating conditions on training within the social platforms to benefit the employees with continuous initiation of awareness activities and events on the forum aligned with social network knowledge on education and the use of technology. In addition, relative to contributing tasks, that is, posting information generally requires less assistance and organizational facilitation. The user typically requires more training and education, that is, finding the correct information efficiently without spending a significant amount of time searching and filtering, and therefore benefits more from a formal support structure. Hence, technical knowledge is necessary for success in the workplace, which is the core of a manager's ability to complete tasks related to widespread information technology knowledge. Their concrete forms are the leading indicators of the employee's expertise. Technical skills are usually very concrete and tangible, and it is easy to teach and learn and even test them (Chin et al., 2020). One way to improve nonprofits' success rate is to increase their leaders' management skills. There is a recognized need for nonprofit managers to have the business knowledge and skills to adapt market-based business practices to their organizations' needs. Essentially, philanthropic efforts help the community, which calls for nonprofit leaders to improve the organization's sustainability and ability to grow and change societal needs in complex, changing environments (Thomas & Van Slyke, 2019).

Training is the set of guidance to involve the employees to achieve their desired results. Technical training is a sequence of instructions, techniques, and expertise to improve employee skills to achieve the expected targets. Employees who are not fully competent are always hesitant to perform any job activity and continue their work with low competency. Technical training could be essential to enhance employee job-related satisfaction and align with effectiveness to achieve the desired results. Technical training provides a comprehensive view of the job tasks to pick up the areas and techniques needed to improve to achieve the required program success. Training in the latest updated working style and technology is also required. It is crucial to have adequate know-how about the changing technology for the new and existing managers. Technical training enhances the managers to run the programs to perform their job tasks successfully and efficiently. Technical training is one of the essential tools to achieve organizational targets, and it is one of the factors that significantly supports nonprofit organizations. (Alvi et al., 2020).

Improving employee working knowledge is essential for nonprofits where managers can perform at their full potential with ongoing training sessions and programs. Training is a consistent set of guidelines to improve functional ability and achieve desired results. Training is a sequence of instructions, techniques, and expertise to enhance the managers' skills to achieve the expected targets where the employees need to be more fully competent and motivated. In contrast, in that case, they are always hesitant to carry on the job activity. Managers' training provides a comprehensive view of the job tasks to pick up the areas and techniques needed to be improved with the latest updated working style and technology. The significant importance of training is that efforts are required to perform the job and organizational tasks effectively to achieve the desired results. Although, it argued that training only provides results as the organization perceives regarding the implication of sources like money, effort, and time. The study suggested that training is one of the essential tools for achieving organizational targets, which is a very supportive factor for organizations (Watad, 2019).

Organizational learning is a long-term change that may lead to inadequate learning capabilities constraining change efforts. In a case study examining organizational learning during the project implementation, the complexity of the interactions between the elements moderating the project implementation efforts and organizational learning attributes. On the one hand, during information technology introduction, nonprofit change can provide management learning opportunities to nonprofit managers through increased data, tools, and professional development programs. On the other hand, it can threaten managers' opportunities for learning by a narrow focus on specific data management skills and information technology-related goals. Post-implementation evaluations of IT-enabled change efforts become essential in building the organizational capacity for learning and knowledge creation to reduce the negative consequences of information technology-enabled change efforts. Feedback mechanisms that inform decision-makers on the usefulness of newly implemented systems in enhancing nonprofit capabilities are also crucial (Watad, 2019).

Nonprofit learning is a process of detecting and correcting errors with the ability of management to identify and fix the planned objectives to yield actual results that will enhance learning is called single-loop learning. However, when management begins questioning and discovering the underlying policies, it will reach double-loop learning, where often the double-loop is at the expense of their clients. Nonprofits create and manage two types of knowledge called explicit and tacit. Explicit knowledge is static and can be documented or stored in a database. Tacit knowledge is knowledge held by human beings based on insights, experiences, emotions, and interactions. Managing tacit knowledge entails nurturing and managing the employees who possess this knowledge.

Through the interaction between managers and their environment, knowledge is created. Knowledge is also created through the dynamic interaction between tacit and explicit knowledge rather than from either one alone. Knowledge creation is non-linear, interactive, and iterative, whereas when explicit knowledge is accessed and acted upon, it becomes tacit knowledge. This process involves the learning-by-doing approach, in

50

which the explicit knowledge is internalized as tacit knowledge in an employee's mind. When practiced, it broadens the learning spiral of knowledge creation. In this context, introducing information technology will affect the relationship between explicit and tacit knowledge in the nonprofit. It will emphasize explicit knowledge creation in the short term by capturing and storing tacit knowledge to become explicit and accessible to managers. For example, learning to do a job is achieved mainly through interacting with others and discussing matters with fellow employees. The project teams create and develop specialized knowledge while completing the work. When this technical knowledge is shared with others, the nonprofits benefit from the competitive advantage. Researchers and practitioners agree that most learning occurs at the intersections of collaboration and cooperation among managers (Watad, 2019).

Knowledge controls managers' technology that organizations use to communicate effectively is typically related to and derived from experience. Explicit articulated, codified, and communicated knowledge so that other people can use this knowledge to work more efficiently. Knowledge creation, that is, development of new or enhancement of existing knowledge or storage, that is, converting knowledge into an explicit form. Transfer in exchange of expertise between nonprofit units (Haamann & Basten, 2019).

**Training**

UTAUT training (facilitating conditions) is expressed by how the managers perceive the entire organization's support in learning to use high technology. The study's participants currently work in a high-technology context (Barchielli et al., 2021) in formalized training that nonprofits may find hiring a consultant or pre-packaged purchase training. Nonprofits should also examine the feasibility of developing a consortium of businesses that could all use the same training. Shared development expenses can be for e-learning, and it can also be done for any training development, thus becoming affordable for nonprofits. E-learning is now an option that provides a template for developing online learning where nonprofits get affordable training tailored to their needs. Many e-learning opportunities are now available (Coroban et al., 2020).

The five principles of systems thinking consider the following principles:

- *Purposefulness*: The goal is to capture why the managers do what they do with big data technology.

- *Composition:* Reach the proper compromise among seemingly contradictory needs and interdependencies.

- *Connectedness:* Understand the behavior and value of the big data within its ecosystem that influences the ecosystem on technology.

- *Perspective:* Try to see where actions intended for one outcome cause the opposite results for big data.

- *Emergence:* Interactions within big data can yield additional capabilities and values that are only sometimes apparent upon first consideration.

The above principles are applied to diverse design efforts (Mieke van der Bijl-Brouwer, & Bridget Malcolm, 2020). Regardless of the method, on-the-job training can be performed by team leaders, trainers, or mentors. On-the-job training is more informal and can be applied immediately. The advantage of on-the-job training is that the manager works, learns, and at the same time gains professional experience. Off-the-job training can be realized both within and outside the nonprofits. Within the nonprofit, the training is carried out in equipped training spaces or centers, and trainers can be nonprofit managers and specialists within the nonprofit providing educational services. Outside the organization, the training is held at the headquarters of educational service providers and aims to develop professional knowledge and skills (Bîrcă et al., 2020).

Offer courses highly relevant to the realistic environment where inconsistency with the content's reality may lead to irreversible mistakes. Therefore, it is necessary to constantly eliminate or update outdated knowledge points, which requires updating the knowledge. There is a need for learners to have an ability assessment platform, a sustainable curriculum learning platform, and a personalized learning tool (Sha et al., 2020).

**Nonprofit and Learning**

The focus needs to develop skills in intelligence data through learning to train managers. The nonprofit should invest more in training to enable their professionals to make them qualified to perform more efficiently and effectively in generating insights that add value. Such skills and complementarities are necessary for teams to extract value from the data. As a link between individual learning and nonprofit organization-wide learning is instrumental, it is necessary to understand the dynamics of such a relationship (Mauricius et al., 2020).

In some instances, the managers of a nonprofit organization do not act, think, or reflect on their organization's behalf. In contrast, the organizational environment does not provide what is described as learning meadows. Therefore, when learning occurs and knowledge has been acquired, it stays in the individual's mind rather than being diffused into the organization's fabric. In such a situation, managers are identified as carriers where the knowledge leaves when these carriers leave the organization. Building on this idea, the managers, in contrast to learning as active learning connectors, are learning agents who think, inquire, reflect, and act on behalf of the nonprofit. The learning incubators are managers who acquire knowledge but need help to bring it to the organization due to a system or complacency. The learning insulators are disengaged managers and do not participate in learning activities. The nonprofit organization must encourage managers to act as learning connectors and implement measures to facilitate learning meadows that bring learning incubators on board. Finally, identify the learning insulators and put them on track by inquiring into the root cause behind their attitudes and behaviors. Failing to provide for transforming managers learning into facilitating conditions is a missed opportunity and could pose a risk to sustainability or progress (Garad & Gold, 2019).

The relationship between the internal and external environments of learning may transit vertically from individual or group (internal) to community (external) and institutional (internal) to global (external) learning levels. Learning and knowledge focus will likely be interactive, for example, communication and a collaborative guide at the community learning level. In contrast, the global learning level is more transformative, such as attitudinal or value change, and more creatively focused. The relationships embody the importance of both internal and external facilitative environments. The suggestion of learning collaboration with competitors in the external environment aligns with the vertical transition from managers or groups to the community aiming at knowledge transfer. It echoes the idea of the organizational learning practices of implicit or explicit knowledge transfer through applying communities of practice. Hence, we suggest the possible transition from the institutional to the global learning level for creativity and transformative learning. It is particularly significant for a fast-growing and expanding organization to cope with challenges deriving from global trends in the business world to achieve excellence in the competitive environment (Kung et al., 2019).

Managers individually or collectively include work-based learning, simulations, and real-world assessments replicating the business environment. Community partnerships expose real-life scenarios and provide critical insight into their current and future market situation. Although time-consuming for participants and sometimes challenging to maintain, such partnerships and collaborations are becoming increasingly necessary as demand for a work-ready and suitably skilled workforce grows in industry 4.0 (Wrye et al., 2019).

The nonprofit should address these emerging technologies from a sensing-data storage-analyzing and responding-learning perspective. From a business perspective, the sensing-data storage-analyzing-responding-learning cycle needs to be connected to the cycle of emerging technologies. Completing the sensing-data storage-analyzing and responding-learning cycle loop is a critical success factor for nonprofits. Many companies are aware of the potential value of emerging technologies and the digital transformation they need to make (Van Heck, 2019).

**Technology Adoption**

Adopting new technology at a nonprofit level is critical during the early diffusion stage. However, although big data's technological importance has been widely acknowledged for several years, most industries, including nonprofits, are still at an early adoption stage. Many are still exploring the function and capabilities of big data and determining how they would work in their context. Learning to use this complex but valuable technology is now a strategic concern for executives in many nonprofits (Sun et al., 2020).

There needs to be more knowledge and training on data on an organizational level where a shortfall of information leads to short-term, reactive approaches to decision-making rather than long-term, preventative, or predictive maintenance methods. Combining these technological and organizational challenges aggravates adoption of new technologies (Yang & Bayapu, 2020). Another significant tendency in society that reshapes skill requirements is increasing competition. Next, skills obsolescence by market developments occurs when employment in certain occupations or sectors shrinks, forcing workers to move to other occupations or sectors. In this process, they may lose part of their human capital. In addition, workers may be forced to change firms, leading to firm-specific skills obsolescence. Both types of mobility are involuntary and may cause skills obsolescence. This obsolescence is problematic when highly occupation, industry, or company-specific skills (Apergis & Apergis, 2020).

An emerging emphasis on the sustainability factors of the industry 4.0 adoption includes the critical success factor of introducing beyond the digital skills related to environmental and social sustainability identified recently are training and capacity building (Porubčinová & Fidlerová, 2020). The nonprofit retools and trains its employees on the latest data skill sets to stay competitive in a data-driven business ecosystem (Dong & Triche, 2020). Specific technical training programs for end-users demonstrating various data use skills can be developed to maximize open data technology uptake awareness. Workshops allow organizing to disseminate training materials and train potential genuine data users. Available data infrastructures may provide a learning environment to support end-users through demos, open online courses, and audiovisual examples that show how open data technologies can be helpful. Training programs and learning environments expect to empower users of open data technologies, which may lead to increased expectancy of the performance of data users and, subsequently, to a higher intention to use data technologies. Managers rely on this result to justify investments in human, organizational, and technological resources. The resources include user manuals, online FAQs, discussion forums, training sessions, and personal human support (Khechine et al., 2020).

The training and future knowledge data must be drawn from the same data space where a task needs to be learned, or a changed model is rebuilt using newly collected training information, called single task learning or isolated learning. It leads to a fundamental problem with this way of learning, where it does not consider any other related information or previously learned knowledge. Training information for human learning involves background knowledge by accumulating and maintaining the knowledge learned from previous tasks and using it seamlessly to learn new tasks and solve new problems with little data and effort. The goal is to break the exclusive training data by exploring using prior knowledge. To characterize the approach to knowledge sharing depending on reusing the learning knowledge instead of relying solely on the tasks training data. The four main ways of sharing knowledge are found in literature, namely (a) transfer learning, (b) multi-task-learning, (c) lifelong learning, and (d) meta-learning (Amina, 2021).

**Transfer Learning Resources**

Managers' capabilities to transfer knowledge across tasks that aim to improve learning and effectiveness of any transfer learning method depends on the source task and how it relates to the target task. A transfer method would produce positive transfer between appropriately related tasks. In contrast, the negative transfer occurs when the source task is not sufficiently related to the target task or if the transfer method does not leverage the relationship well. Increasing positive transfer and avoiding negative transfer is one of the significant challenges in developing transfer learning. The approach aims to discover what part of the learning in the source can help the structure knowledge for the target. Deep transfer learning, as deep learning has become a ubiquitous technique, and the powerful expressive ability of deep learning has also been leveraged to extract and transfer knowledge, such as the relationships among categories. The popular and effective technique for knowledge transfer in terms of pre-training involves teacher and student networks. Therefore, following human learning can always conduct transitive inference and learning solutions to connect the source and target by one or more intermediate shared factors (Amina, 2021).

**Multitask Learning**

Multitask learning shares the general goal of leveraging knowledge across different tasks. However, unlike transfer learning, there is no distinction between source and target tasks. Multiple related tasks, each with insufficient data to train independently, are learned jointly using a shared representation. The training data from the extra tasks serve as inductive bias, acting as constraints for others, improving general accuracy and learning speed. As a result, the performance of all tasks enhances simultaneously. Recent years have witnessed extensive studies on streaming data, known as online multitask learning, where the training data is in multitasking online learning. Each task is to process sequential data. Multitask knowledge includes supervised learning and unsupervised learning. Generally, two commonly used approaches to multitask learning in deep understanding are hard and soft. Hard parameter sharing implies sharing hidden layers between all tasks, and the output layers differ. Soft parameter sharing gives each task its parameters, where the parameters have a regularized distance to facilitate the sharing of learning (Amina, 2021).

**Lifelong Learning**

The basic idea is that a learner requires to integrate new knowledge and stability to prevent forgetting previous knowledge. The dilemma is that while both are desirable properties, the requirements of stability and plasticity conflict. Stability depends on preserving the structure of representations, and plasticity depends on altering it. Excessive plasticity leads to a problem that dramatically refers to catastrophic forgetting, which means the loss or disruption of previously learned knowledge when a new task is learned. The approach is categorized as continual lifelong learning that embodies a knowledge-sharing process to mitigate catastrophic forgetting. It uses prior knowledge from past observed tasks to help continuously learn new future tasks. The lifelong learning approaches include a strategy to retain previously known knowledge sequentially and a transfer mechanism to selectively transfer that knowledge when learning a new task. By analyzing the lifelong learning literature, it is noted that research in this field has only been carried out extensively recently despite the first pioneering attempts and early speculations. However, recently as most of the limits caused by these factors have been exceeded, lifelong is increasingly becoming an area of scientific contribution. New approaches have emerged, including continual learning and lifelong interactive knowledge learning for chatbots (Amina, 2021).

**Metalearning**

Metalearning, or learning-to-learn, improves learning a new task using meta-knowledge extracted across tasks. In a nutshell, learning-to-learn treats learning tasks as learning examples. It aims to improve the learning algorithm, given the experience of multiple learning episodes. In a metalearning system, we distinguish that the meta-learner learns across episodes, and the inner learner is instantiated and trained inside an episode. The metalearning is tightly linked to the process of collecting and exploiting meta-knowledge. Metaknowledge collecting is performed by extracting algorithm configurations such as hyperparameter settings, pipeline compositions, network architectures, the resulting evaluations, the learned parameters, and measurable properties of the task itself, also known as meta-features. Learning-to-learn is a tool for knowledge sharing rather than reusing knowledge per se to solve other knowledge-sharing scenarios where only a few experiences are available.

The metalearning framework involves extracting sharing features among multiple tasks learned simultaneously using a shared meta-network to capture the metaknowledge of semantic composition and generate the parameters of the task-specific semantic composition metalearning setting. Metalearning and experience for continual learning directly minimize catastrophic interference by learning representations that accelerate future learning and are robust to forgetting under online updates in continual learning (Amina, 2021). The business practices across nonprofits require dynamic changes in the skills possessed by managers. The change in nature of work requires defined facilitating conditions with technical training objectives to improve efficiency in simple manual tasks and provide employees with the relevant knowledge that enhances the ability to perform complex tasks and dynamic jobs knowledge (Maity, 2019).

**Summary and Conclusions**

Managers must further build technological foundations, and, most crucially, research points to the importance of learning functional skills related to big data technology in training. Working in multiskilled teams combines different skills and ultimately leverages them to create value in programs for the nonprofit (Sena et al., 2019). Today's focus on knowledge transfer in organizations, wherein experienced employees train their subordinates or subject matter greenhorns or recruits, demands a proper knowledge management system. Appropriate knowledge documentation can be easily accessible to the target audience, be available for reference or modification when needed, and convert individual knowledge into collective organizational knowledge (Maity, 2019).

Gaining critical business insights by analyzing large sizes of various data is becoming necessary for nonprofits. Hence, recent studies pointed out that there should be a better understanding of the impact of technology on data-driven insight generation, which is the goal of big data technology. Using current and historical data to move from not knowing how to solve an ongoing program problem to understanding it is defined as data-driven insight. Nonprofit managers trying to understand big data can help them understand what is happening now in descriptive insight. Likely to occur in the future with predictive insight. Nonprofits must take action to get optimal results in prescriptive insight (Ghasemaghaei & Calic, 2019).

Accurate anticipation is vital to working in a dynamic labor market, where jobs and skill requirements are no longer static. Anticipation allows managers to gauge which jobs may be at risk and identify the tasks and jobs being created. Lifelong learning would meet the needs of the trends that are currently well underway. Anticipating jobs and providing access to learning demands a complex system involving stakeholders like nonprofits that create work environments that support education and enable employees to engage in extended training periods (The learning organization, 2019).

There is currently a need for highly skilled managers dealing with data to make better decisions. Decision-makers can address this issue by training current managers (Merhi & Bregu, 2020). Finally, the need for skills, knowledge, and training is another crucial social implication from the review. There is a massive demand for data management capabilities among professionals, helping embed new technology (Madanayake & Egbu, 2019). However, the collected information must be completed or corrected in training due to inadequate facilitating conditions. In that case, there is a genuine possibility for error, leading to other sequential problems in adopting big data (Wang, 2019).

It is implementing new digital achievements from big data and acting as the essential factor contributing to developing digital technologies. It means managers can take advantage of the enormous opportunities for training, continuing education, development, and participation in economic and social life. The training system should better equip people with skills and knowledge to meet the requirements of the digital work environment in big data technology and societal knowledge. Therefore, it is necessary to promote the broader use of digital media on big data technology in education. Together with all interested parties in the field of education, it will strive to create a digital learning strategy in big data that will systematically use, expand, and implement the capabilities of digital media in big data to provide high-quality education. Nevertheless, there remain questions about adaptation to the challenges of the digital economy related to the continuous improvement of the level of qualification and the development of new skills in technology (Jafarova, 2020). Chapter 3 describes the research methodology used for the study, the introduction to the research design and rationale, the study target population and sampling procedure details, plans for analysis, an explanation of maintaining threats and ethical concerns, and a summary.

Chapter 3: Research Method

This nonexperimental, survey-based online quantitative study on nonprofit managers' technical training measures the extent of the influence of this training on big data technology use. This study followed a quantitative methodology to help narrow the gap in research between what is not known in relation to the nonprofit manager's technical training on the use of big data technology. Chapter 3 has five sections, the first of which includes the research design and rationale. The second section contains the methodology describing the target population, sample population, analysis, risk to participants, pilot study, procedures for recruitment, and survey instrument. The third section of this chapter includes the data analysis plan, the fourth section has threats to validity and ethical procedures, and the fifth section closes with a summary.

**Research Design and Rationale**

In the study, using UTAUT theoretical framework (Venkatesh et al., 2003), the independent variable is technical training, and the dependent variable is the use of big data technology. The quantitative study captures whether nonprofit managers are trained to use big data technology to manage business operations. The survey results were then averaged for this study and included three phases: survey design, data collection, and analysis of the data (Liakos et al., 2021).

The step-by-step methodology for this study is listed as follows:

1.  A survey was created and published on SurveyMonkey's online platform for participants to access.

2. The participants in the survey were acquired randomly from the SurveyMonkey service, and the invitation was sent from SurveyMonkey to the participants with an embedded link to take the survey.

3. The data was evaluated and measured using the statistical test on nonprofit managers' technology training who do not use big data and use big data to manage business operations.

The approach is based on the established research methodology of Queiroz and Wamba (2019) and Venkatesh et al. (2003) used by researchers to collect and analyze the research data.

## Methodology

### Target Population

The target population comprises senior executives, information technology managers, or business managers working in nonprofit organizations throughout the United States (see Table 1). I used a random sampling approach to collect data from the target population (see Demirel, 2022), in which SurveyMonkey was requested to solicit participants who did participate in this study. According to the U.S. Bureau of Labor Statistics (2022), the total number of nonprofit managers is 1,369,470, equating to 8.6% (see Table 2). According to Ariella (2022), the workforce employed in nonprofits is 16,000,000 throughout the United States. After identifying the target population, the next step is inviting participants to gather data to form a sample population.

**Table 1**

*Nonprofit Target Population*

| Managers | Population | Nonprofit target population |
|---|---|---|
| Computer and information research scientists | 126,700 | 12,670 |
| Computer and information systems managers | 509,100 | 50,910 |
| Financial managers | 730,800 | 73,080 |
| Top executives | 98,100 | 9,810 |
| Total jobs | 1,464,700 | 146,470 |

*Note.* Nonprofits account for roughly 10% of jobs in the United States (U.S. Bureau of

Labor Statistics, 2022).

**Table 2**

*Nonprofit Managers*

| Nonprofit managers | Target population |
|---|---|
| Financial managers | 73,080 |
| Fundraisers | 105,800 |
| Health education specialists and community | 126,700 |
| Public relations and fundraising managers | 98,100 |
| Social and community service managers | 173,700 |
| Social workers | 708,100 |
| Business managers | 1,285,480 |
| | |
| Computer and information systems managers | 50,910 |
| Computer and information research scientists | 12,670 |
| Information technology manager | 63,580 |
| | |
| Top executives | 9,810 |
| Emergency management directors | 10,600 |
| Senior executives | 20,410 |
| | |
| Total nonprofit managers jobs | 1,369,470 |

*Note.* Data retrieved from the U.S. Bureau of Labor Statistics (2022).

**Sample Population**

An online survey was created in SurveyMonkey and distributed randomly to the target population, allowing participants to access questionnaires that I used to collect the results from the built-in online tool within SurveyMonkey. Probability sampling was used to select the sample population randomly to ensure that the overall target population represents a generalization (Beaumont & Émond, 2022). To the sample population computed, an additional 10% of potential participants were added to the sample population total, to mitigate the effects of any data errors because the respondents may have filled the fields incorrectly or accidentally skipped them.

**Power Analysis**

I used an online analysis tool to calculate the random sampling population from the target population This was performed in statskingdom.com using power calculation with a built-in statistical calculator shown in a graphical user interface GUI (Statistics Kingdom, n.d.). The value used in the calculation is a confidence level of 95%, and the error margin corresponds to a value of $\alpha = 1 - 0.95 = 0.05$. Data retrieved from the U.S. Bureau of Labor Statistics (2022) indicates that nonprofit managers have an approximate population of 1,369,470, and the total sample population computed number was 385 (see Appendix C). The survey, conducted in SurveyMonkey, included survey questions to collect data on technical training and big data technology use.

**Risk to Participants**

The following measures were taken to reduce potential risks to participants:

- Upon completion of the survey, the preliminary data review was evaluated by transferring it to the personal computer and stored in an encrypted format.

- The participant's identity was not collected during the survey to safeguard privacy, and the participants could stop the survey at any time.

- Survey data were collected through SurveyMonkey, which protects the anonymity of participants in the survey. Participants' demographic information was collected in the survey: gender, years of experience, age of participants, region, and household income.

- Survey participants' data were securely stored during and after the survey.

**Pilot Study**

Queiroz and Pereira's (2019) survey instrument used in this study had previously been tested for validity and reliability, so a pilot study was not necessary.

**Procedures for Recruitment**

SurveyMonkey was requested to solicit participants to participate in the study, and the target population criteria include participants working in nonprofits throughout the United States. To create a survey in SurveyMonkey, I created an account and chose from the menu by adding the survey questions using a tool that allows building the survey and deploying it to collect data randomly from the target data. A hyperlink URL with a message was created targeting the nonprofit managers to enable recruiting survey participants who are willing to take the survey. SurveyMonkey is considered a trustworthy and credible social networking platform, providing an advantage when collecting respondents for the survey. The survey invitation was sent to the participants in an email with a link to the consent form. A survey introduction describing the purpose of the study's relevant information about a survey was the first part that prospective respondents would interact with and help to decide whether to fill out the questionnaire. The message invitation includes the following:

- the purpose of the study,

- information on the qualification criteria and the confidentiality of survey responses, and

- a link to the survey on SurveyMonkey.

The survey's closed-ended questions elicited responses from survey participants on a Likert scale. To edit previous responses, participants could use the back button to review previous sections. The participants were marked as completed on the online survey questionnaire when they clicked submit, and follow-up interviews were unnecessary. The survey questionnaire is an survey instrument comprised of a set of questions to ask the participants in the survey to collect quantitative data. The exclusion criteria include the participants who did not complete the survey or had errors.

**Survey Instrumentation**

In this study, I requested and obtained permission from Queiroz and Pereira (2019, see Appendix B) to use the study's instrument and survey questions, which are supported by the UTAUT. This survey instrument, developed by Queiroz and Pereira, was originally taken from the UTAUT theoretical framework (Venkatesh et al., 2003) on which this research is based. The web-based questionnaire was grounded on UTAUT constructs and has been validated by previous studies (Venkatesh et al., 2003).

Reliability and validity testing for the UTAUT model was sufficient for this study because the survey questions are reused from the UTAUT. The instrument used by Queiroz and Pereira (2019) has exceeded the 0.70 threshold recommended in the literature (Hair et al., 2017), showing the main measures for reliability and validity consistency in the study. Before collecting data, Queiroz and Pereira performed a pilot test with five senior academics and five professionals. Both Cronbach's alpha value and composite reliability were above the 0.70 threshold, and all average variance extracted values were above the 0.50 threshold. Therefore, the reliability and internal consistency measures have been validated. Queiroz and Pereira's survey instrument is adapted from the original survey developed by Venkatesh et al. (2003) in the UTAUT to the understanding of technology adoption.

### Data Analysis Plan

The study's hypothesis appears in the data analysis plan before data collection, which ensures that data analysis is hypothesis-driven instead of data-driven. Before beginning data collection, I created a data analysis plan and outlined clear hypotheses to reduce bias (see Pownall, 2020). The survey excludes any anomalies, such as incomplete or missing data that contain errors that were eliminated because the respondents may have filled the fields incorrectly or accidentally skipped them. Therefore, the result did not involve editing the research data points that may hamper the credibility of the results. The statistical analysis is based on the assumption of normality of the outcome-dependent variable to define whether the distribution is normal in conducting the analysis and whether any outliers are screened out (Haardörfer, 2019). The survey's closed-ended questions measure the construct of the UTAUT model (Venkatesh et al., 2003). A 7-point

Likert scale (1 = *strongly disagree* to 7 = *strongly agree*) was used to collect survey

participant responses that are consistent with measuring the UTAUT model construct

(Venkatesh et al., 2003). Participants could select one response from the 7-point Likert

scale, which allowed the scores to be calculated.

The UTAUT predictor variable technical training (facilitating conditions) is

investigated using questionnaires for survey participants in a survey (Garone et al., 2019)

that will focus on shedding new light on this research. Prior research shows that impacts

may exist in training and the use of technology (Mills & Harris, 2019). Independent

variable technology training (facilitating conditions) is measured with responses to the

following items, as developed by Queiroz and Pereira (2019):

1. I have the necessary technical training and resources to use big data
   technology.

2. I need the necessary technical training and resources to use big data
   technology.

3. Big data technology technical training and resources are compatible with other
   technologies I use.

4. I can get help by acquiring technical training and resources when I have
   difficulties using big data technology.

The UTAUT (Venkatesh et al., 2003) theoretical lens is used due to its powerful

explanatory power and robustness in predicting that nonprofit managers use the

technology in a nonprofit organizational setting (Chin et al., 2019). Responses to the following items in the surveys are a measure of the dependent variable nonprofit

managers who use big data technology:

1. I will not use big data technology.

2. I plan to use big data technology in the future.

3. I'm using big data technology. (Queiroz & Pereira, 2019)

The survey includes the demographic information on the data gathered from

research participants necessary to determine whether the individuals in the study are a

representative sample of the target population for generalization purposes. The survey

questionnaire contains demographic information that includes gender, years of

experience, age of participants, region, and household income.

**Statistics**

A statistical test was used to determine whether the population description has a

normal distribution, and linear regression was used to find the relationship between the

independent and dependent variables. I then transferred the survey data into SPSS

(Version 28) to run the correlation and linear regression to determine whether the sample

data was the same as in the target population. Pearson correlation and linear regression

were used to examine the relationship and how the independent variable affects the

dependent variable. Pearson's correlation coefficient ($r$) measured the numeric values

associated with each closed-ended response. Running regression allows testing the

relationship between the independent and dependent variables on the strength of the

relationship (Wang et al., 2020), and the regression results accept or fail to accept the null

hypothesis. The results were analyzed for statistical significance for the independent and dependent variables of the UTAUT. A correlation was calculated for a relationship between independent and dependent variables that range from +1 to -1. A value near -1 indicates a weak correlation, while a value near +1.0 indicates a stronger correlation between dependent and independent variables (Arif et al., 2018). A list of the survey questions was used to address the research problem that ensures that the survey question, the study's purpose, and the concepts are aligned, and the statistical test was conducted to thoroughly examine the dataset (Frankfort-Nachmias et al., 2020) to find.

- normal distribution of the independent variable,
- correlation between the variables,
- effect size strength of the relationship,
- Analysis of variance (ANOVA) test to statistically assess the equality of means, and
- coefficients strength of linearity.

SPSS (Version 28) was used to average the data and create the graphs and tables that are represented to show the results of the statistical tests. The test for normality was conducted to indicate that the tests for assumptions required for linear regression are sufficient in continuing with the hypothesis testing.

**Hypothesis Testing**

The five basic steps in hypothesis testing (Frankfort-Nachmias et al., 2020) were conducted.

73

1. Making assumptions involves the level of measurement of the variable, the method of sampling, and the shape of the population distribution to allow for the conclusion from the results correctly.

2. Stating the research and null hypothesis and selecting alpha involves the level of significance given at 5% or $\alpha = 0.05$. If the $p$ value is equal to or less than alpha ($\alpha$), evidence supports the null hypothesis that the result is statistically significant. If the $p$ value is greater than alpha ($\alpha$), evidence supports the null hypothesis that the result is not statistically significant.

3. Selecting the sampling distribution and specifying the test statistics involves the normal distribution shown in histogram.

4. Computing the test statistics involves the $p$ value calculated to be $p <$ value.

5. Making a decision and interpreting the results, since the $p$ value is less than alpha ($\alpha$), the evidence against the null hypothesis is that result is statistically significant.

Hypothesis testing is used to determine whether the null hypothesis that the difference in the mean is 0 and an alternate hypothesis that the difference in the mean is different from 0. Understanding the insights with good reliability of representativeness, correlations, and linear regressions allows us to assess relationships between variables without manipulating the independent variable to measure and understand the statistics. The study addressed the following research question and hypotheses:

Research Question - How do nonprofit managers differ in technical training (facilitating conditions) using big data technology compared to managers who have not used big data technology to manage business operations?

$H_0$: Nonprofit managers differ in technical training (facilitating conditions) do-not-use big data technology to manage business operations.

$H_a$: Nonprofit managers differ in technical training (facilitating conditions) do-use big data technology to manage business operations.

## Threats to Validity

### External Validity

According to this study's objectives, external validity refers to whether the results are generalizable (Fabrigar et al., 2020). The threats to external validity include testing reactivity, interaction effects of selection and experimental variables, specificity of variables, reactive effects of experimental arrangements, and multiple-treatment interference. Testing reactivity is a threat to external validity that occurs in response to self-report measures if research participants report the measure during a task (Beauchaine et al., 2019). In this study, testing reactivity is not a threat because the study does not involve changing behavior in some way to observe.

Interaction effects of selection and experimental variables are defined as when the participants in the study are systematically different from others in the general population (Gim, 2019). This study does not threaten the interaction effects of selection because of the absence of pre and post-test studies. The specificity of variables involves it when it is challenging to identify the procedures to which the variables are generalized (Wells &

Clark, 2019). In this study, this is not applicable. Reactive effects of experimental arrangements are when the control involves conditions that cannot be replicated and generalized to the non-experimental. In this study reactive effects of experimental arrangements are not applicable. Multiple-treatment interference involves exposing the subjects to multiple treatments (Barrette, 2019). In this study multiple-treatment interference is not applicable.

**Internal Validity**

Internal validity is the extent to which a research design includes enough control of the conditions and experiences of participants that it can demonstrate an unambiguous explanation for a manipulation. The level of control in a research design directly relates to internal validity or the extent to which the research design can demonstrate control. Nonexperimental research designs typically have the least control on research and, therefore, the lowest threat to internal validity (Lin et al., 2021). The threats to internal validity include history, maturation, testing, instrumentation, statistical regression, experimental mortality, and selection-maturation interaction.

Internal validity to history involves when outside events influence the participants in one compared to the other, and the internal validity is threatened (Slocum et al., 2022). Since the study is not longitudinal, studies are not looking at variables over an extended period. Threat to internal validity due to the maturation effect within the participants systematically varying with time (Kirby et al., 2021). The survey participants in this study do not vary over time.

The threat to internal validity is due to testing when the survey participants learn about the pretest and change the given response (Halili, 2021), and in the study, there are no pre and post-test. The threat to internal validity due to instrumentation is when the biases are due to changes in the instrument over time. Due to instrumentation, a threat to internal validity is whether the instrument is reliable and responsible for the outcome (Kalkbrenner, 2021). The survey instrument will not change and was approved by (Queiroz & Wamba, 2019).

Statistical regression involves the natural tendency for extreme scores to regress or move toward the mean (Jake-Schoffman et al., 2021) and can be controlled in statistical analysis. In this study, it is not applicable. Experimental mortality is due to the selective subject loss that results in the participant drops before the survey is complete (Moser et al., 2022). Selection-maturation interaction where the participants have a different maturation rate, and since the study is not longitudinal, that is, studies do not repeatedly observe the same participants over time.

**Construct Validity**

Although the common understanding of construct validity refers to the extent to which a test measures what it purports to measure (Núria & Tennant, 2019). Construct validity describes the effects of measurement errors on theoretical relationships among constructs if the construct is not valid (Anwar, 2020). Construct validity refers to the extent to which a study's independent and dependent variables correspond to the constructs (Fabrigar et al., 2020). Under the construct method, theoretical considerations are used to optimize the construct validity (Oosterveld et al., 2019). Thus, no threats to the stated statistical construct validity may arise in this study UTAUT (Venkatesh et al., 2003).

## Ethical Procedures

The quantitative study addresses how business managers in nonprofit organizations differ in training, which may affect the understanding of the use of big data technology. Before collecting the responses from the survey issued to the participants, the Walden University Institutional Review Board (IRB) approval was obtained. The Walden University IRB guidelines were followed to eliminate any risk to participants subject to this study. The Walden University IRB approval was acquired to ensure that all United States federal guidelines were observed. Respondents could cancel the survey at any time without risk of inclusion. Although no ethical violations exist in this study, the participants were notified that their responses would be kept anonymous. As required by Walden University, the data collected was encrypted and stored for at least 5 years. No other ethical issues are involved in this study, including the environment, conflict of interest or power differentials, and justification for using incentives.

## Summary

Chapter 3 showed a nonexperimental quantitative study best suited to explaining the exact details of the research design provided to address the research question. Criteria for recruiting survey participants, protection of the participants required by Walden University, operationalization within UTAUT constructs to research design, methodology, and data analysis plan. The results and findings of the study will be explained in Chapter 4.

Chapter 4: Results

This section includes the study's results with a detailed explanation of how a nonexperimental, survey-based online quantitative study on nonprofit managers' technical training measures the extent of influence the big data technology use in business operations (Persaud, 2021). The data were collected using the Measurement Items (Queiroz & Pereira, 2019) survey instrument from the survey participants who were presented with closed-end questions. The summary result is based on average data presented in gathering evidence on the hypothesis to answer the research question. This chapter interprets the research questions with supportive hypotheses based on the statistics for relevant results. The statistical results are analyzed whether the independent variable technical training predicts the dependent variable use of big data technology (Venkatesh et al., 2003). Using the UTAUT model as the theoretical framework, the results were presented by addressing the following research question and hypotheses:

Research Question - How do nonprofit managers differ in technical training (facilitating conditions) using big data technology compared to managers who have not used big data technology to manage business operations?

$H_0$: Nonprofit managers differ in technical training (facilitating conditions) do-not-use big data technology to manage business operations.

$H_a$: Nonprofit managers differ in technical training (facilitating conditions) do-use big data technology to manage business operations.

## Data Collection

The data were collected from participants using the SurveyMonkey platform based on the UTAUT-based survey instrument developed by Queiroz and Pereira (2019). The survey instrument called Measurement Items Queiroz and Pereira (2019; see Appendix D) was used to make the research impactful and avoid erroneous conclusions. Before distributing the survey to the participants, I obtained Walden University IRB approval number 03-03-23-0724019 for this study. The survey invitation was sent to the participants in an email with a link to the consent form. The information in the consent form included that (a) the recruitment of participants in the survey from SurveyMonkey was voluntary, (b) the participants could withdraw from the study at any time, (c) the information would be kept anonymous, and (d) I would not ask for the participants' names or contact information.

The quantitative data were collected using closed-ended survey questionnaires, limiting respondents to what they are expected to answer. The respondents specified their level of agreement by selecting the most appropriate option on the 7-point Likert scale that allows measuring the result in numerical values. The scale of measurement used in the Likert scale is continuous and interval scale. The data collection method is categorized as primary data because participants were asked to participate only once to answer the questionnaires. The geographical coverage to gather the data in this study included nonprofit organizations throughout the United States. Therefore, the questionnaires were suitable to be hosted online since the survey could easily reach many participants.

According to Takumi and Taro (2021), online surveys, such as through SurveyMonkey, play a significant role in research due to the readily available internet to the U.S. population. The use of online surveys is effective because of the advantages of (a) economy, (b) convenience, (c) simplicity, and (d) speed, and participants can review their responses and change them before submission. Seshadri and Broekemier (2022) have described that web-based surveys for nonprofit managers may result in lower responses because of internet security concerns related to receiving spam emails. The evidence pointed to lower responses for online surveys than for traditional paper-based surveys. Therefore, surveys are hosted in SurveyMonkey, which allows strict security by avoiding any safety concerns when conducting the survey online.

The factors that I considered when choosing data collection to increase the chances of achieving effective results for the research questions include the (a) research goal, (b) scope of the study, (c) sample size, (d) data type, (e) survey time, (f) web interface user-friendliness to the participants, (g) online security, and (h) study within the theoretical framework (see Mwita, 2022). This study does not involve triangulation, which refers to using more than one data collection method to offer insights from multiple data collection methods, including confirming whether the instrument will provide similar findings.

The survey started in SurveyMonkey on March 5, 2023, to reach a goal of the total number calculated sample population in (see Appendix C) PowerG ($N = 385$). The data collection from the survey lasted until March 11, 2023, with the total number of participants being 408. The survey result excluded any errors caused by incomplete or missing data that respondents have filled in incorrectly. In this case, the answers were not edited, and 23 surveys were omitted due to errors observed after the examination. The final sample population resulted in 385, which met the minimum required for this study, and the data were exported into SPSS (Version 28).

## Study Results

Correlation and linear regression evaluate the relationship between the dependent and independent variables (Frankfort-Nachmias et al., 2020). The independent variable in this study was technical training, and the dependent variable was the use of big data technology. The level of measurement for the variables was continuous with an interval scale. The unit of analysis was nonprofit managers.

### Baseline Descriptive Statistics

The univariate analysis was conducted to measure central tendency and the patterns surrounding the mean and mode defined by a single value representing the center distribution in the sample collected. Table 3 shows that both variables used in the study have an equal sample size of 385, the standard deviation is less than the mean, and a low standard deviation indicates that data is clustered around the mean.

**Table 3**

*Baseline Descriptive Statistics*

| Statistic | | Use of big data technology | Technical training |
|---|---|---|---|
| *N* | Valid | 385 | 385 |
| | Missing | 0 | 0 |
| Mean | | 3.9359 | 4.1351 |
| Median | | 4.0000 | 4.2500 |
| Mode | | 4.00 | 4.00 |
| Std. deviation | | .84262 | 1.18336 |
| Skewness | | -.308 | -.875 |
| Std. error of skewness | | .124 | .124 |

### Central Tendency

Table 3 indicates that the Skewness = -0.875 for technical training and the Skewness = -0.308 for the use of big data, which are both zeros; therefore, the measure for the central tendency is the mean = 4.1351 for technical training, and the mean= 3.9359 for the use of big data.

### Median and Mode

In Table 3, the SPSS statistics reported that the middle value found by ordering from lowest to highest value is the Median = 4.0 for using big data technology and Median = 4.25 for the technical training. The number that repeated the most often within a data set is Mode = 4.0 is the same for both the use of big data technology and technical training.

### Descriptive Statistics

Demographic information includes gender, years of experience, age of participants, region, and household income. The gender of the participants (see Table 4) presents female participants (73.5%, $n = 283$) being a larger group than male participants (26.5%, $n = 102$).

**Table 4**

*Gender Distribution*

| Gender of participants | $n$ | % |
|---|---|---|
| Male | 102 | 26.5 |
| Female | 283 | 73.5 |
| Total | 385 | 100.0 |

The participants' experience of using big data technology in nonprofit organizations (see Table 5) shows that those with less than 1 year made up a significant percentage (42.3%), followed by those with 1 to 3 years (15.8%). In the survey, the least number of participants with experience in big data technology is 13 to 15 years (2.6%).

**Table 5**

*Years of Experience Using Big Data Technology*

| Years of experience | $n$ | % |
|---|---|---|
| Less than 1 year | 163 | 42.3 |
| 1–3 years | 61 | 15.8 |
| 4–6 years | 38 | 9.9 |
| 7–9 years | 28 | 7.3 |
| 10–12 years | 28 | 7.3 |
| 13–15 years | 10 | 2.6 |
| 15+ years | 57 | 14.8 |

As for the age of the participants (see Table 6), participants aged 41–50 made up the largest group (22.1%, $n = 85$) of survey participants, followed by those aged 31–40 (21.6%, $n = 83$). Ages 26–30 comprised the fewest participants (7.0%, $n = 27$).

**Table 6**

*Age of Participants*

| Age group | n | % |
|---|---|---|
| 18-25 | 35 | 9.1 |
| 26-30 | 27 | 7.0 |
| 31-40 | 83 | 21.6 |
| 41-50 | 85 | 22.1 |
| 51-55 | 36 | 9.4 |
| 56-60 | 43 | 11.2 |
| 60+ | 76 | 19.7 |

The geographical distribution throughout the United States allows focusing on regions where participants are located (see Figure 1). The East North Central region has a significant percentage (20.26%) of participants, followed by the Mid Atlantic (17.92%). New England has the fewest participants (5.19%). The geographical distribution shows the involvement of the nonprofit by region.

**Figure 1**

*Bar Chart by Participants in U.S. Regions*

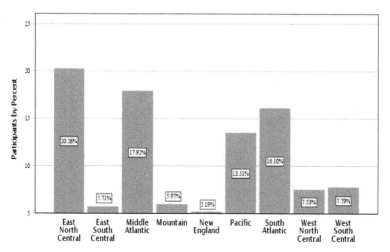

Household income was used to evaluate the socioeconomic status of the

participants, and Table 7 shows the majority are concentrated in the range of $25,000 to

$49,000, followed by $50,000 to $79,999, with the fewest earning $175,000 to $199,999.

Household income shows that the participant's socioeconomic status impacts the

availability of technology. Socioeconomic household income indicates facilitating access

to technology (Phibbs & Rahman, 2022) in using big data.

**Table 7**

*Household Income of Participants*

| Income range | n | % |
|---|---|---|
| $0-$9,999 | 24 | 6.2 |
| $10,000-$24,999 | 18 | 4.7 |
| $25,000-$49,999 | 99 | 25.7 |
| $50,000-$74,999 | 89 | 23.1 |
| $75,000-$99,999 | 51 | 13.2 |
| $100,000-$124,999 | 31 | 8.1 |
| $125,000-$149,999 | 19 | 4.9 |
| $150,000-$174,999 | 11 | 2.9 |
| $175,000-$199,999 | 6 | 1.6 |
| $200,000+ | 13 | 3.4 |
| Prefer not to answer | 24 | 6.2 |

**Summary of Descriptive Statistics**

The female (73.5%) nonprofit managers throughout the United States are the

majority of survey respondents. The most common age group among respondents is 41-

50 years (22.1%). Many participants are new to big data technology with less than one

year of experience (42.3%). The socioeconomic status describes the household income concentration between the range of \$25,000 to \$49,000, and they are actively involved in East North Central (20.26%) significant percentage, followed by Mid Atlantic (17.92%).

**Normal Distribution**

In Figure 2, the histogram shows the plotted point distribution close to a straight line at a 45-degree angle, bell-shaped and symmetric around the mean. It indicates the independent variable *technical training* and shows that the distribution is approximately normal, indicating normality.

**Figure 2**

*Histogram for Technical Training*

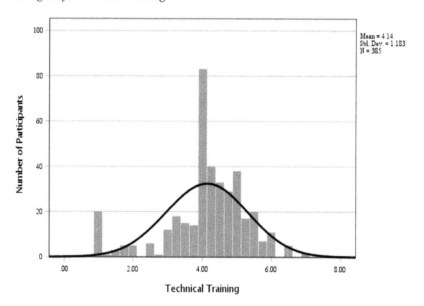

**Hypothesis Testing**

Hypothesis testing involves rejecting or failing to reject the null hypothesis. Rejecting the null hypothesis means the *p* value falls below the alpha value 5% level of significance, that is, $\alpha = 0.05$, indicating the results are statistically significant, which means a predictive relationship exists between the technical training and the use of big data technology. The correlation determines the strength and direction of the relationship between technical training and the use of big data technology. Bivariate regression describes whether technical training influences the use of big data technology (Laureate Education, 2016b).

**Scoring**

Since the internal consistency through Cronbach's alpha value was more than 0.5, all questions implicitly measure the same latent construct (Queiroz & Pereira, 2019). The scores measured in the Likert scale are averaged for four independent variable surveys (see Appendix D) questions (Q7, Q8, Q9, and Q10) to get one independent variable technical training score for each participant. Likewise, the Likert scores on three dependent variable survey questions (Q4, Q5, and Q6) are averaged to get one dependent variable score use of big data technology for each participant (Queiroz & Pereira, 2019).

**Correlation**

Pearson correlation was conducted in SPSS (Version 28), with both variables having an interval measurement scale. Table 8 has a significance level at 5% or $\alpha = 0.05$, the $p < .001$. Since the $p$ value is less than alpha, evidence against the null hypothesis that the result is statistically significant, the correlation coefficient ($r$) ranges between -1 and +1, and Pearson correlation coefficient ($r = 0.580$) indicates a moderate relationship between technical training and the use of big data technology. The classification used for correlation values (positive or negative) is as follows: very weak (0.0–0.19), weak (0.20–

0.39), moderate (0.40–0.69), strong (0.70–0.89), and very strong (0.90–1.00) (Orleno

Marques da et al., 2020, p. 4).

**Table 8**

*Correlations*

|  |  | Use of big data technology | Technical training |
|---|---|---|---|
| Use of big data technology | Pearson correlation | 1 | .580** |
|  | Sig. (2-tailed) |  | <.001 |
|  | N | 385 | 385 |
| Technical training | Pearson correlation | .580** | 1 |
|  | Sig. (2-tailed) | <.001 |  |
|  | N | 385 | 385 |

** Correlation is significant at the 0.01 level (2-tailed).

**Model Summary and Effect Size**

In Table 9, the positive Pearson correlation coefficient (r) represents the direction of the relationship. A positive correlation signifies that if technical training goes up, then using big data technology will also go up. The R-squared value determines the effect size of= 0.336 is the quality of fit of the technical training associated with big data technology. Adjusted R-squared determines the reliability of the correlation and how much is determined by the addition of technical training. The standard error of the estimate measures the accuracy of predictions or precision. The standard error of estimate value of= 0.68756 indicates data variability.

**Table 9**

*Model Summary*

| Mode l | R | R square | Adjusted R square | Std. error of the estimate |
|---|---|---|---|---|
| 1 | .580[a] | .336 | .334 | .68756 |

a. Predictors: (Constant), Technical training.

**ANOVA Test**

In Table 10, a large F-statistics is the variation among group mean has a higher value indicating evidence against the null hypothesis indicating that result is statistically significant and $p$-value less alpha ($\alpha$) having statistical significance regression model, $F (1, 383) = 193.726, p < 0.001$.

**Table 10**

*Analysis of Variance (ANOVA)[a]*

| | Model | SS | df | MS | F | Sig. |
|---|---|---|---|---|---|---|
| 1 | Regression | 91.582 | 1 | 91.582 | 193.726 | <.001[b] |
| | Residual | 181.060 | 383 | .473 | | |
| | Total | 272.642 | 384 | | | |

[a] Dependent variable: Use of big data technology.
[b] Predictors: (Constant), Technical training.

**Coefficients**

In Table 11, The correlation coefficient is a statistical measure of the strength of a linear relationship where beta $\beta$ indicates that for every unit increase in technical training, the use of big data technology increases by 0.413 units. The larger $t$-value and the smaller $p$-value (Sig) show evidence against the null hypothesis.

**Table 11**

*Coefficients*[a]

| Model | Unstandardized coefficients | | Standardized coefficients | | |
|---|---|---|---|---|---|
| | B | SE | Beta | t | Sig. |
| 1 (Constant) | 2.229 | .128 | | 17.484 | <.001 |
| Technical training | .413 | .030 | .580 | 13.919 | <.001 |

[a] Dependent Variable: Use of big data technology.

**Visual Plot Chart**

The regression equation y= a + b*x, where y is the dependent variable *use of big data technology* on the y-axis, x is the independent variable *technical training* plotted on the x-axis, "b" in Table 11 has a value of= 0.58 which is the slope of the line and "a" has a value of= 2.229 of is the y-intercept, therefore y= a + b*x = 2.229 + 0.58 * x. In Figure 3, the regression indicates a positive correlation of an upward slope on a scatterplot between the *use of big data technology* and *technical training.*

**Figure 3**

*Plot Chart*

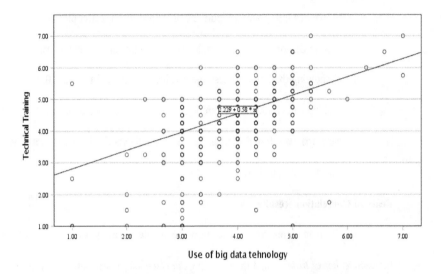

**Five Steps in Hypothesis Testing**

The five basic steps in hypothesis testing (Frankfort-Nachmias et al., 2020, p. 248) are as follows:

1. Making assumptions: A random sample was used for technical training and use of big data technology and had a sample size of= 385. Both variables, technical training and the use of big data technology are measured on an interval level of measurement. The collected sample satisfies the required sample size of 385.

2. Stating the research and null hypothesis and selecting alpha: The level of significance is given at 5% or $\alpha = 0.05$. Compare the P-value against ($\alpha$).

3. Selecting the sampling distribution and specifying the test statistics: The normal distribution for technical training and use of big data technology is shown in a histogram in Figure 2 bell-shaped and a scatter plot in Figure 3 straight diagonal line. The p-value is used to test the null hypothesis.

4. Computing the test statistics: The p-value is calculated to be $p < 0.01$.

5. Making a decision and interpreting the results: Since the p-value is less than alpha ($\alpha$), therefore fails to accept the Ho null hypothesis, and the result is statistically significant.

**Pearson Correlation Results**

The Pearson correlation coefficient was computed to assess the linear relationship between *technical training* and the *use of big data technology*. Pearson correlation coefficients range in value from $-1$ (a perfect negative relationship) to $+1$ (a perfect positive relationship) (Burgund et al., 2023). Pearson correlation draws a line and specifies how far away the data points are from the best-fit line. The level of significance is given at 5% or $\alpha = 0.05$. In Table 8, the $p < 0.001$. Since the $p$ value is less than alpha ($\alpha$), the evidence against the Ho null hypothesis is that the result is statistically significant, thus rejecting that nonprofit managers differ in technical training (facilitating conditions) do-not use big data technology to manage business operations. The Pearson correlation is positive, $r = 0.58$, N = 385, $p = 0.001$. The Pearson correlation results indicated a significantly moderate association between technical training and the use of big data technology ($r(385) = 0.58$, $p < 0.001$), indicating that the greater the proportion of *technical training*, the greater the *use of big data technology*, therefore, variable *technical training* influences the *use of big data technology*.

## Summary

Chapter 4 analyzes the statistical results related to technical training (independent variables), which influences the use of big data technology (dependent variable). The chapter provided descriptive data and summarized the Pearson correlation and linear regression results. The regression model results show that for every unit increase in the technical training, the use of big data technology increases by units 0.413. The evidence was against the null hypothesis that the result was statistically significant and accepted the alternate hypothesis. Chapter 5 continues with detailed, in-depth analyses of the results, including the discussion, conclusions, and recommendations.

Chapter 5: Discussion, Conclusions, and Recommendations

The purpose of this nonexperimental survey-based study is to examine whether

nonprofit managers' technical training may influence the use of big data technology in

business operations. The research design involved a plan to respond to the research

problem within the UTAUT theoretical framework (Venkatesh et al., 2003). For data

collection, participants were provided with a structured survey instrument based on

UTAUT (see Appendix D) adapted from Queiroz and Pereira (2019). Chapter 5

summarizes the results from the analysis of the data collected. This chapter provides the

interpretation of the findings, limitations of the study summary, recommendations,

implications, and conclusion.

## Interpretation of Findings

### Peer-Reviewed Literature

In Industry 4.0, with technological advances, the nonprofit needs to adjust to the

revolution by adapting to the new demands in technical training so the managers can get

up to speed with serving the community (Cunha et al., 2020). Nonprofit managers require

the necessary technical knowledge and skills in the social environment in which they

operate so they can work efficiently in different environments and collaborate. Technical

training on using big data technology can enhance the manager's skills to run programs

that support the community so they can function effectively. Nonprofit managers must

gain insights into becoming knowledgeable about society (Karaatmaca et al., 2021)

through technical training on big data technology to meet the organization's mission.

Technical training on big data needs a plan of action to meet society's requirements so it establishes nonprofit growth and evolution (Xu et al., 2022).

**Descriptive Statistics Results**

The responses gathered on the gender from the survey questionnaire on demographics show that female nonprofit managers were in the majority carrying out community support within the resources that significantly influence nonprofits' activities, practices, and strategic leadership decisions in business operations that benefit society (Öberg, 2021). Results show that nonprofit managers have less than one year of experience in big data technology. Persaud (2021) stated that nonprofit managers require cognitive and technical skills with at least 2 to 3 years of experience with having strong technical knowledge and experience in big data technologies that allow them to demonstrate an understanding of the practical applications. Results indicate that nonprofit managers need technical training in big data technology that can lead to avoiding accidents in gathering inaccurate information and narrowing down the mismatch between the manager's skills and knowledge demand.

Nonprofit managers in the age group 41–50 are the most numerous and are likely less tech-savvy compared to the younger generations and may require technical training to update their essential skills and gain knowledge to keep up with the latest big data technological advancements to manage the nonprofit's programs. The age group shows that nonprofit managers are professionals and have a strong work ethic to be employed in nonprofit organizations (Douglas & Roberts, 2020) but need to improve in technical skills.

Socioeconomic status based on household income is essential for nonprofit managers to obtain the technological resources at home to adopt big data technology. More advantaged socioeconomic individuals are more likely to have better access to digital technology and more frequently have the skills required to use big data technology (Phibbs & Rahman, 2022). The nonprofits should consider facilitating technical training for the managers in regions with less participation to counter the inequality and adverse desirability effects that require further consideration of managers in these regions impacting the society (Hean, 2022).

**Study Findings**

This research examines whether the predictor variable technical training predicts the dependent variable use of big data technology. The statistical test was conducted to explain the relationship between a dependent variable, the use of big data technology, and an independent variable, technical training. Findings suggest that as technical training increases, knowledge of big data technology also increases. The results indicate a positive relationship between technical training and the use of big data technology. In other words, using big data technology predicts technical training. It means that for every one-unit increase in technical training (one tenth of a standard deviation), the model predicts an increase of 0.413 units using big data technology.

Several studies have shed light on industrial 4.0 technology adoption, but UTAUT theoretical framework training (facilitating conditions) still needs to be researched (Khin & Daisy, 2022). Therefore, this research finding shows that the training (facilitating conditions) positively influences the decision to adopt industrial 4.0 big data technology for nonprofits. Nonprofits need operational resources such as skilled workers who can handle technical knowledge to evaluate the programs. Qualified nonprofit managers with experience and understanding of business operations need technical training from nonprofits to manage the current operations, and all this can be accomplished through technological support, guidance, and training.

## Limitations of the Study

The limitations observed during this research are in addition to those previously identified in Chapter 1. The nonprofit organization size needs to be measured involving small nonprofit organizations involving fewer managers with a wide range of tasks to meet organizational goals. In contrast, large organizations use a high degree of work specialization to operate more efficiently. Most participants have less than one year of experience using big data technology, which shows that the respondents are less tech-savvy and need more technical expertise to understand technology. The survey instrument uses a closed-ended question. Thus, a previously validated instrument is used in the data collection to overcome the limitations. Research findings may not be helpful to nonprofit managers working in other countries who do not share characteristics with U.S. nonprofit organizations.

## Recommendations

Based on the results of this quantitative research study on technical training in the use of big data technology, the following is a list of recommendations for future research:

- Future research can explore the effectiveness of technical training that includes teaching format, learning time, completed history, and evaluation of

the quizzes on the choices for future quick learning in web interfaces or
mobile. Future research can show how big data technology and technical
training are deeply intertwined within different levels of nonprofit
organizations. Evaluate the technological advances driving the need for new
and updated technical skills that need to align efficiency and fast learning
content for nonprofit managers so they can effectively access the learning
material and latest information. Future research can determine training
development needs for managers that indicate a new or improved competency
assessment to help managers understand how their current skills must align
with future nonprofit big data technology. Thus, managers can find a way to
determine what improvements are needed to ensure future success.

- The future researcher can evaluate whether the program has successfully
  achieved targeted goals and whether the program is strongly associated and
  aligned with the overall manager's skills. Future research success depends on
  program insights using big data technology by gathering information about a
  specific program so nonprofits can make informed decisions about that
  program to benefit society. Future researchers could evaluate the embedded
  program cost involved in technical training to gain more detailed learning
  about nonprofit business operations with additional tools and knowledge
  necessary for success. Determine the technical training cost that impacts
  nonprofit managers' productivity and better understand their responsibilities
  and the knowledge and skills they need to do that job.

- Further research should consider artificial intelligence with big data technology that facilitates cognitive decision-making algorithms to mimic human intelligence to perform tasks with up-to-date technical training skills. Artificial intelligence outpaces humans' ability to absorb, interpret, and make complex decisions based on big data technology in nonprofit systems with the latest required training skills in Industry 4.0. Artificial intelligence and big data technology's pursuit of intelligent machines is futuristically providing insights into human intelligence and stimulating technological and scientific innovation that could lead to future societal transformations. In addition to better understanding the value and benefit of using new technology to reform human lives in society and by accepting technology, nonprofits can successfully deliver social programs that allow researchers to understand society's needs and empower a better future. Future studies can validate the study's strength using different nonprofits business operations in different geographic areas.

## Implications

The theoretical framework includes constructs of the UTAUT (Venkatesh et al., 2003). The significance of this study was to add to the existing body of knowledge related to technical training provided to nonprofit managers that influences the use of big data technology. Nonprofit managers getting help with big data technology will operate effectively by gaining insights into serving their community by reducing unemployment, poverty, social exclusion, and low education levels.

**Social Change**

Nonprofit managers are dedicated to helping people by restoring their dignity and quality of life through innovative education and community-driven social interaction. It will be possible by developing skills through training in big data technology that allows serving the community by creating rich, meaningful, actionable data. Using big data allows managers to focus on actionable dashboards that can significantly improve the ability to tell a compelling story related to the mission, increase accountability in business operations, and monitor key trends in social behaviors regarding the health of society. Data is among nonprofit managers' most critical strategic assets, which allows for bringing actionable insights. As big data technology has made data increasingly accessible, data science continues transforming and shaping to solve societal problems.

**Significance to Theory**

The UTAUT expands nonprofit managers' acceptance and use of big data technology by filling a research gap showing a relationship between technical training facilitating conditions and the decision to use and adopt big data technology. Therefore, this study contributed to the UTAUT model (Venkatesh et al., 2003) body of knowledge in illustrating technical training by testing the UTAUT model (Venkatesh et al., 2003) with insights into using big data technology.

Within the framework of UTAUT, providing technical training to nonprofit managers to adopt big data technology allows them to gain knowledge and competence in performing business operations tasks to the best of their ability and get insights into running the programs. The study shows that confidence in technology can lead to increased competency in using information and gaining knowledge with better monitoring of nonprofit business operations. Nonprofit managers need to develop an understanding of technology acceptance by getting technical training that will lead to using the latest technology resources.

Technical training (facilitating conditions) allows the development of the essential knowledge and skills needed to operate big data technology so that managers can apply technical skills to support management activities. Training abridges knowledge and operations by addressing topics that lead to adequate public trust transparency by solving complex problems to generate more significant value for society and lead managers to become highly proficient in the societal program. The study delivers the explanatory power to standard acceptance in UTAUT, which helps support technical training to use big data technology.

**Recommendations for Practice**

In the age of data digitization, nonprofit managers need technical training to understand advances in big data technology that allows learning about the audiences and the needs in the context of the society around them. There are still longstanding problems that nonprofit organizations need to address when faced with societal challenges, including poverty, education, and healthcare, which means still more work to be done using big data technology to create a change. Nonprofit managers need in-house skills in big data technology that allows for developing a sensibility on data connects and influence how to leverage this understanding toward the mission.

For nonprofit managers, technology is vital in developing staff skills to use the technology appropriately. In-house skills in big data technology allow the work to be effectively managed in business operations. With limited resources, nonprofit managers must maximize and double down to align efforts between strategic direction and allocated program funds. All will be attainable by utilizing big data technology to help meet the target audiences' needs.

## Conclusion

The research question is answered: nonprofit managers' technical training influences the use of big data technology in business operations. Technical training allows an understanding of the effective use of big data technology and equips nonprofit managers with the technical know-how to manage business operations. Nonprofit managers can gain confidence by using big data technology that increases productivity and efficiency in accurately obtaining the targeted information on critical social programs. Although fewer studies have shed light on adopting big data technology through Industrial 4.0 training (facilitating conditions), this research indicates that the influence decision to embrace technological advancements will get up-to-date information on social issues (Khin & Kee, 2022).

Technical training and education are the backbones of the economy, and nonprofit managers require well-structured educational infrastructure training to learn how to understand data and adopt big data technology. A nonprofit need to leverage modern big data technology solutions today to avoid falling behind compared to the competition. It is always possible to begin the digital transformation journey by providing education on technical training, which will cultivate a more technology-centric (and competitive) business model. Therefore, there is a need for a dramatic shift in meeting society's expectations in utilizing the practical impact of big data technology that meets the community's needs.